First World

and Army of Occupation

War Diary

France, Belgium and Germany

MW01245666

28 DIVISION
Divisional Troops
Divisional Cyclist Company
28 December 1914 - 31 October 1915

WO95/2271/2

The Naval & Military Press Ltd
www.nmarchive.com
Published in association with The National Archives

Published by

The Naval & Military Press Ltd

Unit 10 Ridgewood Industrial Park,

Uckfield, East Sussex,

TN22 5QE England

Tel: +44 (0) 1825 749494

www.naval-military-press.com

www.nmarchive.com

Contents

28TH DIVL CYCLIST COY.

DEC 1914-OCT 1915

28TH DIVISION
DIVL TROOPS

Instructions regarding War Diaries and Intelligence
Summaries are contained in F. S. Regs., Part II.
and the Staff Manual respectively.   Title pages
will be prepared in manuscript.

Hour, Date, Place	Summary of Events and Information	Remarks and references to Appendices
Page 58 WESTOUTRE. 1915		
July 4th (continued)	to report to R.E. for digging in cable lines	
11. am	Church parade for all men in billets.	
2 pm	Lieut. Packard assisted No. 16 Mobile Vet Section in a range practice on SCHERPENBERG range.	
3 pm	No 3 platoon relieved No 2. at DICKEBUSCH.	
4.30 pm	No. 2 platoon returned.	
6 pm	No 2 platoon returned	
7 pm	Nos. 4 & 5 platoons went to DICKEBUSCH for digging in cable	MP.
July 5th		
3.30 am	Above platoons returned.	
8.30 am	No. 2 platoon proceeded to KEMMEL for digging cable.	
10.30 am	Capt. Agg visited SCHERPENBERG.	
3. pm	No 4 platoon relieved No 3 at DICKEBUSCH	
5.30 pm	Nos 2 and 3 platoons returned to billets.	
7. pm	Nos 5 and 6 platoons went to DICKEBUSCH for digging in cable	MP?
July 6th	Above platoons returned to billets.	
3.40 am	No 3. platoon went to KEMMEL for digging in cable wires.	
8.30 am	No 5 platoon relieved No 4 at DICKEBUSCH, the latter returning to billets at 5 pm.	
3. pm	No 3 platoon returned to billets.	
5.30 pm	Nos 1 and 6 platoons went to DICKEBUSCH for digging in	
7.30 pm	[Cables.	MP.

1247 W 3299 200,000 (E) 8/14 J.P.C. & A.   Forms/C. 2118/11.

Instructions regarding War Diaries and Intelligence Summaries are contained in F. S. Regs., Part II. and the Staff Manual respectively. Title pages will be prepared in manuscript.

Hour, Date, Place	Summary of Events and Information	Remarks and references to Appendices
Page 59 WESTOUTRE		
1915 –		
July 7th		
3·45 am	Nos 1 and 6 platoons returned to billets	
8·30 am	No 4 platoon proceeded to KEMMEL for digging in cables	
10·30 am	Lieut. Packard visited SCHERPENBERG	
3 pm	No 6 platoon relieved No 5 at DICKEBUSCH	
5 pm	No 4 platoon returned	
5·30 pm	No 5 platoon returned.	
7·30 pm	Nos 1 and 2 platoons proceeded to DICKEBUSCH for digging in cable wires	ML
July 8th	Above platoons returned to billets	
3·30 am	No. 5 platoon went to KEMMEL for digging in cable lines.	
8·30 am	Patrol of 2 N.C.O.'s and 4 men of No 1 Platoon proceeded to DICKEBUSCH instead of 1 platoon as heretofore.	
3 p.m.	Nos 6 and 5 platoons returned	
5·30 pm	No 3 platoon proceeded to DICKEBUSCH for digging in wires.	
7·15 pm	50 men from Nos 1 & 2 platoons under Lieut Bugs & Lieut Daniels proceeded to R.E Park DICKEBUSCH to draw tools for digging.	
7·30 pm	The party then marched to cross roads 500 yds W.N.W. of VIERSTRAAT and improved a subsidiary line of trenches running in a northerly direction parallel to the road.	ML

1247 W 3299 200,000 (E) 8/14 J.B.C. & A. Forms/C. 2118/11.

28th Divisional Cyclist Coy:

Vol I. 28. 12. 14 — 31. 1. 15.

WAR DIARY

or

INTELLIGENCE SUMMARY

(Erase heading not required.)

Army Form C. 2118.

28 DIVISIONAL CYCLIST Company-

Instructions regarding War Diaries and Intelligence Summaries are contained in F. S. Regs., Part II. and the Staff Manual respectively. Title pages will be prepared in manuscript.

Hour, Date, Place	Summary of Events and Information	Remarks and references to Appendices

28 December 1914 Winchester —	The 28 Divisional Cyclist Company was formed at Pitt Camp – as follows –
	 O.C. Captain F.J.G. Agg – 1st K.O.Y.L.I.
	 2 Lieutenant Lieut J. A. Jervois – 1st K.O.Y.L.I.
	 Company Sergt Major – J. Lawn ⎫
	 Company Q. M. S. – H. Middleton ⎭ 1st K. O. Y. L I.
	    2 Batmen ⎫
	    5 Signallers ⎪ 1st K. O. Y. L I.
	    2 Artificers ⎪
	    1 Transport Driver ⎭
	 Lieut Packard, 1 Sergt 29 men - 2d Bn Kings own Regt
	 Lieut Gordon Burge – 1 " 29 men - 1st Bn. York & Lancaster Regt
	 Lieut St Claire Bolton 1 " 21 men 1st Bn Suffolk Regt
	 Lieut Greville Williams 21 men 2d Bn Northumberland Fusiliers
	 Lieut Dalton 1 Sergt 29 men 3d Bn Royal Fusiliers	

1247 W 3299 200,000 (E) 8/14 J.B.C. & A. Forms/C. 2118/11.

WAR DIARY
or
INTELLIGENCE SUMMARY
(Erase heading not required.)

Army Form C. 2118.

Instructions regarding War Diaries and Intelligence Summaries are contained in F. S. Regs., Part II. and the Staff Manual respectively. Title pages will be prepared in manuscript.

Hour, Date, Place	Summary of Events and Information	Remarks and references to Appendices
	Lieut H Phillips 1 Sergt 29 men 3ʳᵈ Bn Middlesex Regt	
	1 Sergeant 15 Rank & File 1 Bn Welch Regiment	
	The Company was formed into 6 platoons	
	Consisting of 1 officer 1 Sergeant 29 men –	
	Which were again subdivided into 4 sections	
	of 6 men & 1 N.C.O –	
	Total strength of Company –	
	8 Officers	
	8 S. Sergeant & Sergeants	
	2 Artificers	
	182 Rank & File	

WAR DIARY
or
INTELLIGENCE SUMMARY
(Erase heading not required.)

Instructions regarding War Diaries and Intelligence Summaries are contained in F. S. Regs., Part II. and the Staff Manual respectively. Title pages will be prepared in manuscript.

Page 3

Hour, Date, Place	Summary of Events and Information	Remarks and references to Appendices
29 Dec 1914	Equipping the Company —	Ja
30 " "	" "	Ja
31 " "	" "	Ja
1 Jan 1915	" "	Ja
2 Jan "	" "	Ja
3 " "	" " 2 A.S.C. Drivers attached to the Company	Ja Ja
4 " "	" "	Ja
5 " "	" " "	Ja
6 " "	" " "	Ja
7 " "	" " "	Ja
8 " "	" " 200 Bicycles were drawn from Ordnance	Ja
	4 Heavy 2 Light Draught Horses drawn from Remount Officer	Ja

1247 W 3299 200,000 (E) 8/14 J.B.C. & A. Forms/C. 2118/11.

WAR DIARY

or

INTELLIGENCE SUMMARY

(Erase heading not required.)

Army Form C. 2118.

Instructions regarding War Diaries and Intelligence Summaries are contained in F. S. Regs., Part II. and the Staff Manual respectively. Title pages will be prepared in manuscript.

Hour, Date, Place	Summary of Events and Information	Remarks and references to Appendices
9 January 1915	Equipping the Company —	A
10 " 1915	-- --	A
11 " "	-- --	A
12 " "	Inspection of the 28th Division by H.M. the King.	A
13 " "	Equipping Company exercises under Platoon Commanders	A
14 " "	Parades under Platoon Commanders —	A
15 " "	— do —	
	Lt J a Jervois left WINCHESTER with 5 N.C.O's & 6 Bicycles by Train for SOUTHAMPTON, thence to France for Billetting purposes —	A.
16	trading a Coach equipment	
17	" " do " "	

1247 W 3299 200,000 (E) 8/14 J.B.C. & A. Forms/C. 2118/11.

Instructions regarding War Diaries and Intelligence Summaries are contained in F. S. Regs., Part II. and the Staff Manual respectively. Title pages will be prepared in manuscript.

Page 5

1915

Hour, Date, Place		Summary of Events and Information	Remarks and references to Appendices
18 January	WINCHESTER	Company left PITT CAMP for SOUTHAMPTON.	
	7.30 An		
	12.20 p	arrived SOUTHAMPTON entrained in H.T. "BELLEROPHON"	
	7 pm	left SOUTHAMPTON	
19 January	4 am	arrived off HAVRE.	
	11.30 am	Disembarked at "PONDICHERRY" Quay.	
		Company fitted with warm clothing	
		Company billeted for the night - dock shed	
20 January	4.30 p	Company left Shed for Point T where it entrained with Northumbrian Company R.E.	
	9 pm	Train left for HAZEBROUCK.	
21 January	1.30 am	Train arrived ROUEN	
	9.30 am	Train arrived ABBEVILLE	
		Breakfast issued to Company -	

1247 W 3299 200,000 (E) 8/14 J.B.C. & A. Forms/C. 2118/11.

WAR DIARY
or
INTELLIGENCE SUMMARY
(Erase heading not required.)

Army Form C. 2118.

Instructions regarding War Diaries and Intelligence
Summaries are contained in F. S. Regs., Part II.
and the Staff Manual respectively.   Title pages
will be prepared in manuscript.

Hour, Date, Place	Summary of Events and Information	Remarks and references to Appendices
21 January – Cl. 5/ – HAZEBROUCK 8/pm BORRE 10.30/	Arrived – detrained Arrived & Billeted – 1.2.3 Platoon -- & together – 4,5, 6 " } together + 4 officers – } 4 officers } 1 Catapult } together – 3 Batmen }	
22 January – BORRE	Platoons & Bicycles inspected by Platoon Officer	9a –
23 January – BORRE	Platoon exercised under Platoon Officer –	9a 9a

1247   W 3299   200,000   (E)   8/14   J.B.C. & A.   Forms/C. 2118/11.

WAR DIARY
or
INTELLIGENCE SUMMARY
(*Erase heading not required.*)

Army Form C. 2118.

Instructions regarding War Diaries and Intelligence Summaries are contained in F. S. Regs., Part II. and the Staff Manual respectively. Title pages will be prepared in manuscript.

Hour, Date, Place	Summary of Events and Information	Remarks and references to Appendices
23rd January BORRE. 3.55 p.m.	Three officers patrols despatched to report to G.O.C. 83 Brigade. Lieut Boulton & 6 men ordered to reconnoitre METEREN-BERTHEN - BOESCHERE Lieut Burge + 6 men — BAILLEUL - DICKEBUSH Lieut Williams + 6 men — METEREN - WESTOUTRE	
24th January BORRE 11.45/-	Lieut Boulton returned to Billets —	Fa
6 a.m.	Lieut Williams & patrol returned	Fa
3.40 p.m.	Lieut Burge & patrol returned —	Fa.
25th January BORRE	Platoons exercised under Platoon Officers	Fa
26 January BORRE	do.	Fa
27 January BORRE	do.	Fa.
28th January BORRE	do	Fa.

1247 W 3299 200,000 (E) 8/14 J.B.C. & A.   Forms/C. 2118/11.

WAR DIARY
or
~~INTELLIGENCE SUMMARY~~

(Erase heading not required.)

Army Form C. 2118.

Instructions regarding War Diaries and Intelligence Summaries are contained in F. S. Regs., Part II. and the Staff Manual respectively. Title pages will be prepared in manuscript.

Hour, Date, Place	Summary of Events and Information	Remarks and references to Appendices
29 January – BORRE	Platoons exercised under Platoon Officer Pl.	
30 January – BORRE	do	Pa
31 January – BORRE	do	Pa

31. 1. 15

F. J. G. Agglahr
Cd 28 Divisional Cyclist Coy.

1247 W 3299 200,000 (E) 8/14 J.B.C. & A. Forms/C. 2118/11.

28th Divisional Cyclist Coy.

Vol II . 1 — 28. 2. 15

WAR DIARY

or

INTELLIGENCE SUMMARY

(Erase heading not required.)

Army Form C. 2118.

Instructions regarding War Diaries and Intelligence Summaries are contained in F. S. Regs., Part II. and the Staff Manual respectively. Title pages will be prepared in manuscript.

Hour, Date, Place	Summary of Events and Information	Remarks and references to Appendices
BORREE, February 1st 6.40 a.m	The Company paraded in marching order with one blanket & machintosh sheet on the front of the bicycle, Lack on rear carrier, to proceed to BRAND HOEK, in vicinity of VLAMERTINGHE in accordance with Operation orders – No I. 28th division	*:- The weight in too great for the bicycle – The roads were so bad, it was impossible to ride the bicycle –
8 a.m	BAILLEUL was reached –	
12.30/-	BRANDHOEK. reached –	
	The Company was billeted in three farms – the vicinity	
VLAMERTINGHE	The supply wagon + S.A.A. cart was sent on at 6.30 p.m previous night –	
Feb 2	The Billets were put in sanitary condition they had been previously occupied by French troops –	
Feb 3rd	The Roads in vicinity improved —	
Feb 4	———————— do ———	

1247 W 3299 200,000 (E) 8/14 J.B.C. & A. Forms/C. 2118/11.

WAR DIARY
or
INTELLIGENCE SUMMARY

(Erase heading not required.)

Army Form C. 2118.

Instructions regarding War Diaries and Intelligence
Summaries are contained in F. S. Regs., Part II.
and the Staff Manual respectively. Title pages
will be prepared in manuscript.

Hour, Date, Place	Summary of Events and Information	Remarks and references to Appendices
BRANDHOEK		
February 4 - 1915 -	Telegram received from 28ᵗʰ Divisional Headquarters for	
7.15 p.m.	Company to report at once to G.O.C. 83ʳᵈ Infantry Bde	
7.55 p.	Company left billets with 170 Rds S.A.A. per man — (150 strong)	
	proceeded via VLAMERTINGHE & YPRES to 83ʳᵈ Inf Bde H.Qrs	
	1¼ miles due S. of YPRES, where it arrived 10.20 p.m. —	The roads are very unsuitable
	During the night the Company was utilised in carrying	for bicycle work at night
	up Water, Rations, Ammunition to East Yorkshire Regt	
	Kings Own Lancash Regt, & K.O.Y.L.I. in the trenches —	
February 5ᵗʰ 1915	7 a.m. Ration carrying was completed —	ℳ
	The Company returned to Ypres where bicycles had	
	been left previous night —	
	10 a.m. The Company arrived back in billets —	
		ℳ

WAR DIARY
or
INTELLIGENCE SUMMARY
(Erase heading not required.)

Army Form C. 2118.

Instructions regarding War Diaries and Intelligence
Summaries are contained in F. S. Regs., Part II.
and the Staff Manual respectively. Title pages
will be prepared in manuscript.

Page

Hour, Date, Place	Summary of Events and Information	Remarks and references to Appendices
BRANDHOEK		
February 6	— Platoons exercised under Platoon Commanders Fa —	
February 7	1pm. Instructions received from HdQrs 2 8 Division — to patrol the line of the sequial Company from Divisional Head quarter to Brigade HdQrs — Fa	Orders & map of line marked A. attached.
	9pm No 4 Platoon (ol. & Greville Williams) proceeded on patrol —	
February 8	7.30 am Patrol — No 4 Platoon returned — Nothing to report Fa	
	9am No 3 Platoon (ol. Lt Bolton) patrolled the lines	
	1pm Patrol returned to billets — nothing to report on	
	8.30pm No 3 Platoon proceeded on patrol Fa	
Feb 9	7 am Patrol returned — nothing to report Fa.	

WAR DIARY
or
INTELLIGENCE SUMMARY
(Erase heading not required.)

Army Form C. 2118.

Instructions regarding War Diaries and Intelligence Summaries are contained in F. S. Regs., Part II. and the Staff Manual respectively. Title pages will be prepared in manuscript.

Hour, Date, Place		Summary of Events and Information	Remarks and references to Appendices
1915			
BRANDHOEK			
February 9	8 am	No 5 Platoon (O.C. 2 Lieut Dalton) proceeded on Patrol	
	12.30 p	Patrol returned —	
	8 p.m	Patrol left billets —	
February 10th	7 a.m	Night Patrol returned. nothing to report —	A
	8.30 a.m	No 6 Platoon (O.C. 2 Lieut Phillips) proceeded on Patrol —	
	1 p —	Patrol returned —	
	8.30 p.m	Night Patrol (No6) left Billets —	A
February 11	7.30 a.m	Night Patrol returned nothing to report —	
	8.15 am	No 1 Platoon (O.C. Lieut Packard) proceeded on Patrol —	
	12.45 p	Patrol returned —	
	7.30 p	Night Patrols (No1) left Billets —	A

1247 W 3299 200,000 (E) 8/14 J.B.C. & A. Forms/C. 2118/11.

WAR DIARY

or

INTELLIGENCE SUMMARY

(Erase heading not required.)

Army Form C. 2118.

Instructions regarding War Diaries and Intelligence Summaries are contained in F. S. Regs., Part II. and the Staff Manual respectively. Title pages will be prepared in manuscript.

Hour, Date, Place	Summary of Events and Information	Remarks and references to Appendices
BRANDHOEK - 1915.		
February - 11th	O.C. Company with patrol visited 83 Inf. Bde H.Qrs + country in vicinity, nothing to report -	
February 12 -	7.30a. Night patrol (No. 1) returned to billet, nothing to report -	5p.m - 10p.m - Fa
	8.15a. No 2 Platoon (O.C. Lieut Burge) proceeded on Patrol	
	12.30p. Patrol returned -	
	6p - Night Patrols (No 2 P.) left Billets -	Fa
February 13th -	8.a.m Night Patrols returned, nothing to report -	
	8.30.. No 3 Platoon (O.C. Lieut Bolton) proceeded on Patrol	
	1 p.m. Patrol returned	
	6.30p. Night Patrol (No. 3 P.) left Billets -	
February 14	6a - Night Patrol returned, nothing to report -	Fa
	8.30a. No 4 Platoon (2Lt Lt Greville Williams) proceeded on Patrol -	Fa

WAR DIARY
or
INTELLIGENCE SUMMARY
(Erase heading not required.)

Army Form C. 2118.

Instructions regarding War Diaries and Intelligence
Summaries are contained in F. S. Regs., Part II.
and the Staff Manual respectively.   Title pages
will be prepared in manuscript.

Part 14

Hour, Date, Place	Summary of Events and Information	Remarks and references to Appendices
BRANDHOEK - 1915		
2ᴺᴰ YPRES.		
February 14 — 12.30pm	Patrol returned —	
4pm	Night Patrol (No 4. P) left Billets —	9a —
February 15 — 6a	Night Patrol returned — nothing to report	9a
8.30a	No 5 Platoon (O.C. 2 Lieut Dalton) proceeded on	
	Patrol —	
1.15pm	Patrol returned —	
6pm	Night Patrol (No 5 P) left Billets —	9a
February 16 — 7a	" " " returned, nothing to report	9a
9am	No 6 Platoon (O.C. Lieut Phillips) proceeded	
	on patrol	
12.30a	Patrol returned	
7pm	Night Patrol (No 6 P) left Billets	
11.25pm	Message received from Divisional Head quarters	
	to take the Company to that centre —	9a

WAR DIARY
or
INTELLIGENCE SUMMARY
(Erase heading not required.)

Army Form C. 2118.

Instructions regarding War Diaries and Intelligence Summaries are contained in F. S. Regs., Part II. and the Staff Manual respectively. Title pages will be prepared in manuscript.

Hour, Date, Place	Summary of Events and Information	Remarks and references to Appendices
BRAND HOEK - — nr. YPRES. February 17.		
12.10 a.m	The Company left Billets	
12.55 a.m	The Company arrived Divisional Hd Qrs - Instruction received to report to G.O.C. 84th Infantry Brigade on YPRES - LILLE Road -	
2.15 a.m	Arrived - 84th Bde Hd Qrs - Instruction received to proceed to Wood - S. of Canal d'YPRES. 500 x due E. of ECLUSE. No.7. & hold Southern edge of wood covering footbridge across Canal -	
3 a.m	Arrived at the wood & took up position. The Cheshire Regiment on our arrival took up rations to the Suffolk regiment in the trenches - We received no casualties -	
6 a.m	Message received from 84th Bde Hd Qrs to withdraw on return of Cheshire Regiment to N. bank of Canal - & report at Bde Head Quarters -	
7 a.m	Reported at Bde Hd Qrs - & instructed to return to Billets -	

1247 W 3299 200,000 (E) 8/14 J.B.C. & A. Forms/C. 2118/11.

WAR DIARY
or
INTELLIGENCE SUMMARY
(Erase heading not required.)

Army Form C. 2118.

Instructions regarding War Diaries and Intelligence
Summaries are contained in F. S. Regs., Part II.
and the Staff Manual respectively. Title pages
will be prepared in manuscript.

Hour, Date, Place	Summary of Events and Information	Remarks and references to Appendices
BRANDHOEK - & ½ YPRES - Feby 17 - 8-15a.	The Company arrived back in billets -	
6 a.m	The night patrols returned -	
	Numbers One + two Platoons did night patrol -	
Feby 18th 6p --12MN.	Number one Platoon under Lt Packard on patrol	Ja
12.5a - 7am	Number two Platoon under. Lt Burge -	
	Nothing unusual to report -	
	6p --12MN. Number 3 Platoon under Lieut Bolton. found patrols	
	No unusual occurrence to report -	Ja
Feby 19a 12.5a - 7a -	Number 4 Platoon under Lieut Williams a patrol	
	No unusual occurrence to report -	
6p --12MN	Number 5 Platoon under Lieut Dalton on patrol	Ja
	No unusual occurrence to report	
Feby 20b 12-5a - 7a -	Number 6 Platoon under Lieut Phillips on patrol	
	No unusual occurrence to report -	Ja

Instructions regarding War Diaries and Intelligence Summaries are contained in F. S. Regs., Part II. and the Staff Manual respectively. Title pages will be prepared in manuscript.

Page 17

Hour, Date, Place	Summary of Events and Information	Remarks and references to Appendices
BRANDHOEK - N⁰ YPRES		
February 20 - 6 pm - 12 MN	Number 2 Platoon under Lieut Burge on patrol no unusual occurrence to report -	
February 21ˢᵗ 12·5 am - 7 am	Number 1 Platoon under Lieut Packard on patrol no unusual occurrence to report -	Do
6 pm - 12 MN	Number 4 Platoon under Lieut Williams on patrol no unusual occurrence to report -	Do
February 22ⁿᵈ 12·5 a - 7 a	Number 3 Platoon under Sergt Bumstead on patrol no unusual occurrence to report -	
February 22ⁿᵈ 6 pm - 12 MN	Number 6 Platoon under Lieut Phillips on patrol no unusual occurrence to report -	Do
February 23ʳᵈ 12·5 a - 7 a	Number 5 Platoon under Lieut Dalton on patrol no unusual occurrence to report -	Do

WAR DIARY
or
INTELLIGENCE SUMMARY

(Erase heading not required.)

Army Form C. 2118.

Instructions regarding War Diaries and Intelligence
Summaries are contained in F. S. Regs., Part II.
and the Staff Manual respectively.   Title pages
will be prepared in manuscript.

Page 18

Hour, Date, Place	Summary of Events and Information	Remarks and references to Appendices
BRANDHOEK – nr YPRES – February 23rd – 6p.m + 12 MN	No 1 Platoon under Lieut Packard went on Patrol. nothing to report –	9a
Febry 24 – 12·5a – 7a	No 2 Platoon under Lieut Burge went on Patrol nothing to report	
6p – 12 MN	No 3 Platoon under Lieut Servos went on Patrol nothing to report	
February 25 – 12·5a – 7a	No 4 Platoon under Lieut William went on Patrol – nothing to report – Except one civilian who was found without a pass. He was confined – Guardroom at YPRES –	9a
6p – 12 MN	No 5 Platoon under Lieut Dalton went on Patrol nothing to report.	9a
Febry 26 – 12·5a – 7a	No 6 Platoon under Lt Phillips went on Patrol nothing to report.	
6p – 12 MN	No 2 Platoon under Lieut Burge went on Patrol nothing to report except one civilian found nr YPRES without a pass – He was confined in Guard room –	9a

WAR DIARY
or
INTELLIGENCE SUMMARY
(Erase heading not required.)

Army Form C. 2118.

Instructions regarding War Diaries and Intelligence
Summaries are contained in F. S. Regs., Part II.
and the Staff Manual respectively. Title pages
will be prepared in manuscript.

Hour, Date, Place	Summary of Events and Information	Remarks and references to Appendices
Page 19 BRANDHOEK 2ⁿᵈ YPRES. February 27 – 12.5 a. – 7 a. –	No 1 Platoon under Lieut Packard went on patrol – nothing to report	9a
6 p. – 12 M.N.	No 4 Platoon under Lieut. Williams went on patrol nothing to report –	9a
February 28th 12.5 a. – 7 a. –	No 3 Platoon under Lieut. Bolton went on patrol – nothing to report	
6 p. – 12 M.N.	No 6 Platoon under Lieut Phillips went on patrol nothing to report –	9a –
	J H Agglehite Cy 28 Div Cyclist Coy	
1-3-15 –		

Operation Orders - No I

by Capt A.J. ... of 28 Squadron

I. The Company will ... daily to the support of ... the aeroplane & telegraph wires ... support Company for the wires ... have been properly ... by ... squad.

II. The line will be installed as far ... to the 28 Bde Advanced Hd Qrs.
(a) 28° Bde Hd Qrs
(b) 3rd Advanced Hd Qr (28 Bde) & 84 Bde Hd Qr
(c)   "   " 85   "   "
If 83 Bde ... + ... forming line to their Hd Qrs.

III. The Platoon will be divided into 4 parties who will be no shown on attached map —

IV. Platoons will each one party out during ... + ... patrols out at night. The same procedure for night patrols will be given to take ...

...
A.J. ...
of 28 Squadron
8.2.15

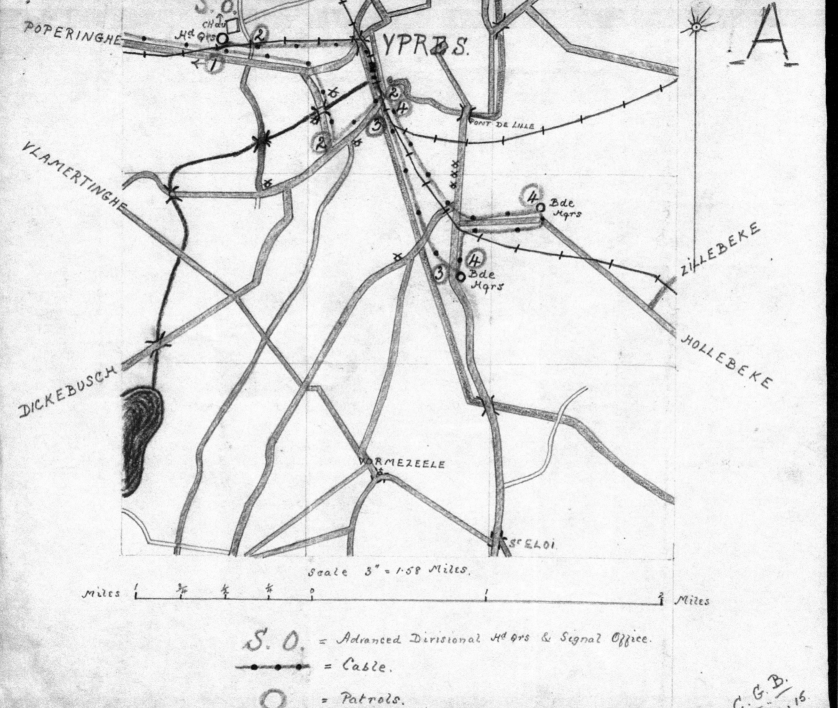

S.O.

POPERINGHE

CH au
Hd Qrs

YPRES.

2

1

PONT DE LILLE

VLAMERTINGHE

2

3

4

4

Bde
Hqrs

ZILLEBEKE

4

Bde
Hqrs

3

HOLLEBEKE

DICKEBUSCH

VORMEZEELE

St ELOI.

Scale 3" = 1·58 Miles.

Miles 1   3/4   1/2   1/4   0   1   2 Miles

S. O. = Advanced Divisional Hd Qrs & Signal Office.

⏤•⏤•⏤ = Cable.

◯ = Patrols.

C. G. B.
10·2·15.

28th Div.l Cyclist Coy:

Vol III   1 – 31. 3. 15.

Nil

WAR DIARY
or
INTELLIGENCE SUMMARY
(Erase heading not required.)

Army Form C. 2118.

Hour, Date, Place	Summary of Events and Information	Remarks and references to Appendices
BRANDHOEK nr YPRES March 1st 12.5am –7a	No 5 Platoon under Lieut Dalton on patrol – Nothing to report. Oc 28 Divisional Cycle Company appointed Camp Commandant of Hut Town – VLAMERTINGHE. He moved to the Brigade Headquarters on the VLAMERTINGHE – OUDERDOM Road –	Fa
6f–12 M.N.	No 1 Platoon under Lieut Packard on patrol – Nothing to report	
March 2nd 12.5a–7a	No 2 Platoon under Lieut Burge on patrol Nothing to report –	
7–10p –	Message received from HdQrs 28 Division to send 100 men to report at 9th Bde Headquarters, to be employed in building trenches –	
9–5p –	Arrived Bde Headquarters – drew pick & shovel & proceeded to M.1. Trench –	Fa

Instructions regarding War Diaries and Intelligence
Summaries are contained in F. S. Regs., Part II.
and the Staff Manual respectively.   Title pages
will be prepared in manuscript.

Page 21

Hour, Date, Place	Summary of Events and Information	Remarks and references to Appendices
BRANDHOEK Nr YPRES. March 3rd		
3.45 a.m.	Work completed at the trench –	
	Casualties during the night. Two men wounded –	
5.15 a.m.	The Company arrived back at their billets –	
2 p.m.	Nos. 1 & 2 Platoons & headquarter of the Company moved to Bde Hd Qrs Hut Town by VLAMERTINGHE.	
5.30 p.	Message received that the Company was to report at 9th Bde Hd Qrs at 8 p. – for trench work –	
6.30 p.	Company left Billets –	
8 p. –	Company arrived at Bde Hd Qrs & proceeded to M.1. trench & carried on with the previous nights' work –	
March 3rd 4/3/15	6 p.m. – 7 a –	No 3 Platoon a patrol under Lieut Bolton Nothing to report

Instructions regarding War Diaries and Intelligence Summaries are contained in F. S. Regs., Part II. and the Staff Manual respectively. Title pages will be prepared in manuscript.

Page 22

Hour, Date, Place	Summary of Events and Information	Remarks and references to Appendices
VLAMERTINGHE March 4th — 2.45a.	Company completed work in trench & returned to Billets — Casualties during the night = Two men wounded	FA —
March . 5 6pm to 5am	No 4 Platoon a patrol under Lieut Williams — Were reported out at . ECLUSE . No 9 . No's 1 & 2 Platoon employed as working party at the Hutments, clearing the area & improving roads —	FA —
March 5 6pm to March 6" 6am	No 5 Platoon a patrol under Lieut Dalton — Nothing to report — No's . 1 & 2 Platoon assisting R.E. at hutments	FA
6pm. 6am - 7.3.15	No 6 Platoon a patrol under Lieut Williams. Nothing to report —	FA

WAR DIARY
or
INTELLIGENCE SUMMARY

Army Form C. 2118.

(Erase heading not required.)

Instructions regarding War Diaries and Intelligence
Summaries are contained in F. S. Regs., Part II.
and the Staff Manual respectively. Title pages
will be prepared in manuscript.

Part

Hour, Date, Place	Summary of Events and Information	Remarks and references to Appendices
March 7th 6 p — to 6 a.m. 8.3.15	No 3 Platoon. Lt Bolth on patrol nothing to report. —	Ja
March 8 6 p — to 6 a.m. 9.3.15	No 4 Platoon under Lt Williams on patrol. nothing to report. —	Ja
March 9 6 p — to 6 a.m. 10.3.15	No 5 Platoon under Lt Dalton on patrol. nothing to report. —	Ja
March 10 6 p — to 6 a.m. 11.3.15	No 6 Platoon under Lt. Phillips on patrol. nothing to report. —	Ja
March 11 6 p — 6 a.m. 12.3.15	No 3 Platoon under Lieut Bumstead on patrol. — nothing to report.	Ja

Instructions regarding War Diaries and Intelligence
Summaries are contained in F. S. Regs., Part II.
and the Staff Manual respectively.   Title pages
will be prepared in manuscript.

Page 24 Hour, Date, Place 1915	Summary of Events and Information	Remarks and references to Appendices
March 12 – 6p – to 6a – 13.3.15	No 4 Platoon under Lieut. Williams on patrol – nothing to report –	do
March 13 – 6p.m to 6a – 14.3.15	No 5 Platoon under Lieut Dalton patrol. nothing to report –	do
March 14 – 6p – to 6a – 15.3.15	No 6 Platoon under Lieut Phillips on patrol – nothing to report –	do
March 15 – 6p – to 6a – 16.3.15	No 3 Platoon under Sergt Bumstead on patrol. nothing to report –	do
March 16 6p – to 6a – 17.3.15	No 4 Platoon under Lieut Williams on patrol – nothing to report	do

1247 W 3299 200,000 (E) 8/14 J.B.C. & A.   Forms/C.2118/11.

WAR DIARY
or
INTELLIGENCE SUMMARY

Army Form C. 2118.

Instructions regarding War Diaries and Intelligence
Summaries are contained in F. S. Regs., Part II.
and the Staff Manual respectively. Title pages
will be prepared in manuscript.

(Erase heading not required.)

Page 25

Hour, Date, Place	Summary of Events and Information	Remarks and references to Appendices
VLAMERTINGHE		
March 17 — 6p — to 6a. 18.3.15	No 5 Platoon under Lt Dalton on patrol — Nothing to report —	✓
March 18 — 6p — to 6a. 19.3.15	No 6 Platoon under Lt Phillips on patrol — Nothing to report	✓
March 19 — 9.30p	Nos. 3, 4, 5 & 6 Platoons moved from Billets to Huts ' —	✓
6p — to 6a. 20.3.15	No 4 Platoon on Patrol under Lt Williams Nothing to report —	✓
March 20 — 6p — to 6a. 21.3.15	No 5 Platoon under Lieut Dalton on patrol nothing to report.	✓
March 21 — 6p — to 6a. 22.3.15	No 6 Platoon under Lieut Phillips on patrol nothing to report.	✓

WAR DIARY
or
INTELLIGENCE SUMMARY
(Erase heading not required.)

Army Form C. 2118.

Instructions regarding War Diaries and Intelligence
Summaries are contained in F. S. Regs., Part II.
and the Staff Manual respectively. Title pages
will be prepared in manuscript.

Hour, Date, Place	Summary of Events and Information	Remarks and references to Appendices
VLAMERTINGHE		
March 22nd 6p- to 6a- 23.3.15	No 1 Platoon under Lt Packard on patrol — Nothing to report	Fa
March 23r 6p- to 6a- 24.3.15	No 2 Platoon under Lt Bridge on patrol — Nothing to report —	Fa
March 24 6p- to 15 6a- 25.3.15	No 3. Platoon under Sergt Bumstead on patrol Nothing to report —	Fa
March 25 — 6p- to 6a- 26-3-15	No 4 Platoon under Lieut Williams on patrol Nothing to report —	Fa
March 26 6p- to 6a- 27.3.15	No 5. Platoon under Lieut Dalton on patrol Nothing to report —	Fa
March 27 — 6p- to 6a- 28-3-15	No 6 Platoon under Lieut Phillih on patrol Nothing to report	Fa

Instructions regarding War Diaries and Intelligence Summaries are contained in F. S. Regs., Part II. and the Staff Manual respectively. Title pages will be prepared in manuscript.

Page 27	Hour, Date, Place	Summary of Events and Information	Remarks and references to Appendices
	VLAMERTINGHE 1915		
March 28th	6h — to 6a. 29.3.15	No 1 Platoon on Patrol under Lieut Packard — nothing to report —	✓a.
March 29	6h — to 6a. 30.3.15	No 2 Platoon on Patrol under Lieut Burge — nothing to report —	✓a
March 30	6h — to 6a. 31.3.15	No 3 Platoon on Patrol under Serjt Burnstead — nothing to report.	✓a
March 31	6p.m. — to 6a. 1.4.15	No 4 Platoon on Patrol under St. Jervois — nothing to report —	✓a

J.J. Applant
Cdg 28 Divisional Cyclist Coy

1/4/15

1247 W 3299 200,000 (E) 8/14 J.B.C. & A.   Forms/C. 2118/11.

25th Div.l Cyclist Coy:

Vol IV 1 – 30.4.15.

WAR DIARY
or
INTELLIGENCE SUMMARY
(Erase heading not required.)

Army Form C. 2118.

Instructions regarding War Diaries and Intelligence Summaries are contained in F. S. Regs., Part II. and the Staff Manual respectively. Title pages will be prepared in manuscript.

Paf Af

28

Hour, Date, Place	Summary of Events and Information	Remarks and references to Appendices
VLAMERTINGHE 1915		
April 1st 6p.— t 6a 2-4-15	No 5 Platoon on patrol under Lieut Dalton — Nothing to report —	da
April 2 6p.— t 6a 3-4-15	No 6 Platoon on patrol under Lieut Phillips Nothing to report	da
April 3rd 6p.— t 6a 4-4-15	No 1. Platoon on patrol under Lieut Packard— Nothing to report—	da.
April 4 6p— t 6a 5-4-15	No 2. Platoon on patrol under Lieut Burge — Nothing to report —	da.
April 5 6p— t 6a 6-4-15	No 3 Platoon on patrol under Sergt Brunstead Nothing to report—	da

WAR DIARY
or
INTELLIGENCE SUMMARY
(Erase heading not required.)

Army Form C. 2118.

Instructions regarding War Diaries and Intelligence
Summaries are contained in F. S. Regs., Part II.
and the Staff Manual respectively.   Title pages
will be prepared in manuscript.

Page 27

Hour, Date, Place	Summary of Events and Information	Remarks and references to Appendices
VLAMERTINGHE		
1915 April 6ᵃ 6pm to 6a. 7.4.15	No 4 Platoon & patrol under Lieut. Wilham — Nothing to report	da
April 7ᵗ 6pm to 6a. 8.4.15	No 5 Platoon patrol under Lieut Dalton — Nothing. to report —	da
April 8ᵗ 6p to 6a. 9.4.15	No 6. Platoon & patrol under Lieut Phillips Nothing to report —	da.
April 9ᵗ 6p to 6a. 10.4.15	No 1. Platoon & patrol under Lieut Packard — Nothing to report	da.
April 10ᵗ .	Patrols withdrawn on handing over the area to Vᵗ Division p	
April 11ᵗ .	O.C. 2 Cyclists handed over duties of Camp Commandant to Staff Captain 13ᵗ Brigade	da.

Instructions regarding War Diaries and Intelligence
Summaries are contained in F. S. Regs., Part II.
and the Staff Manual respectively.   Title pages
will be prepared in manuscript.

Page
30

Hour, Date, Place	Summary of Events and Information	Remarks and references to Appendices
VLAMERTINGHE.		
April 12th	Cyclist moved into the farm & vacated the huts	Do
11.30p	Zeppelin passed over huts & dropped 10 bombs	
	no damage was done	Do.
April 13th	9a — Cyclist Company moved into farms — N. of VLAMERTINGHE. 800ˣ	Do.
	50 men sent to clean — Château — Comte. de PARC.	Do
April 14th	— Fatigue party — 80 men clean Château	Do.
April 15th	— Fatigue party 80 men cleaning Château	Do.
	All officers reconnoitred the area between YPRES and LONNEBEKE & made maps of area —	Do

Instructions regarding War Diaries and Intelligence Summaries are contained in F. S. Regs., Part II. and the Staff Manual respectively. Title pages will be prepared in manuscript.

(Erase heading not required.)

Part 3¹

Hour, Date, Place	Summary of Events and Information	Remarks and references to Appendices
VLAMERTINGHE-- 1915. April 16.	Fatigue party cleaning Château	do.
April 17-	Fatigue party cleaning Château	do.
	Reconnoitred the ground & trenches between YPRES & ZONNEBEKE	da
	Cyclist officers moved from farm into billet at CHATEAU on account of a case of Typhoid occurring at the farm —	da.
April 18ᵘ.	Capt. F. J. Agg proceeded to YPRES and took over the duties of Assistant Provost Marshal.	FJS.
April 19ᵘ.	Lt. Dalton and Lt Phillips with party of Six men from No 5. and Six men from No 6 platoon reconnoitred approaches to 2ⁿᵈ and 3ʳᵈ Line of trenches between YPRES and ZONNEBEKE, Also the Southern sector of YPRES, in order that the men could be employed as guides.	FJS

Instructions regarding War Diaries and Intelligence
Summaries are contained in F. S. Regs., Part II.
and the Staff Manual respectively.   Title pages
will be prepared in manuscript.

Page 3

Hour, Date, Place	Summary of Events and Information	Remarks and references to Appendices
VLAMERTINGHE		
April 20th	I reconnoitred roads N of YPRES with No 3 platoon, and Lt Williams with No 4.	Sd
	Company and 3 officers moved into billets at the VLAMERTINGHE Schools at 3 p.m.	Sd
April 21st 3 p.m	3 officers and the interpreter moved into billets in VLAMERTINGHE.	
	Lt Pack and with No 1 platoon and Lieut Benge with No 2 platoon reconnoitred roads N of YPRES.	Sd
	Draft for the company of 1 Sergeant and 27 other ranks arrived at VLAMERTINGHE station at 2.15 p.m.	Sd
April 22nd 2.15 p.m		Sd
5.45 p.m	At 6.45 p.m received orders from 28th Division that the company was to leave billets in VLAMERTINGHE and proceed to Headquarters of the Division at the Chateau VLAMERTINGHE. Arrived at H.Q at 7.35 p.m.	Sd
	Transport was sent to POPERINGHE via	

1247 W 3299 200,000 (E) 8/14 J.B.C. & A.   Forms/C. 2118/11.

Instructions regarding War Diaries and Intelligence
Summaries are contained in F. S. Regs., Part II.
and the Staff Manual respectively.   Title pages
will be prepared in manuscript.

Hour, Date, Place	Summary of Events and Information	Remarks and references to Appendices
Page 33 VLAMERTINGHE April 22nd	OUDERDOM and RENINGHELST.	Sel
9 p.m	At 9 p.m received orders from 28th Division to send one officer and platoon to report to Col Fodder at St JEAN: to reconnoitre and report on position of the left of the Canadian Division, and to reconnoitre along the canal banks in a Northern direction Lieut Packard and No 1 platoon left at	Sel. Sel.
9.10 p.m	9.10 p.m	
10 p.m	At 10 p.m I sent Lieut Benge and No 2 platoon to report to O.C 366th Battery R.F.A. To patrol in front of the battery.	Sel.
10.15 p.m	At 10.15 p.m remainder of company moved into palm house about 300x E of Chateau	Sel.

1247 W 3299 200,000 (E) 8/14 J.B.C. & A.   Forms/C. 2118/11.

Instructions regarding War Diaries and Intelligence
Summaries are contained in F. S. Regs., Part II.
and the Staff Manual respectively. Title pages
will be prepared in manuscript.

Hour, Date, Place	Summary of Events and Information	Remarks and references to Appendices
POST 3H VLAMERTINGHE		
April 23rd 9.45 a.m	At 9.45 a.m I sent Lieut Williams and No4 platoon to relieve Lieut Packard at St JEAN.	Yes
11.10 a.m	At 11.10 am Lieut Packard and platoon returned.	Yes
8 p.m	At 8 p.m I sent Sergeant Pellet and Six men to report to O.C. 8th Middlesex for duty as orderlies.	Yes
April 24th 5.40 a.m	Orderlies from 8th Middlesex returned at 5.40 a.m	Yes
10 a.m	At 10 a.m I sent Lieut Dalton and platoon to relieve Lt. Williams.	Yes
10.15 a.m	At 10.15 a.m I sent Lieut Phillips and a patrol to reconnoitre state of roads in YPRES.	Yes

WAR DIARY
or
INTELLIGENCE SUMMARY
(Erase heading not required.)

Army Form C. 2118.

Instructions regarding War Diaries and Intelligence
Summaries are contained in F. S. Regs., Part II.
and the Staff Manual respectively. Title pages
will be prepared in manuscript.

Page 36

Hour, Date, Place	Summary of Events and Information	Remarks and references to Appendices
VLAMERTINGHE.		
April 24. 11.45 am	Patrol returned at 11.45 a.m and reported all roads passable for transport.	Yes
12.20 pm	Lieut Williams and platoon returned at 12.20 pm.	Yes
3 pm	At 3 pm I sent Lieut Packard and platoon to report to 85th Bde Headquarters at VERLORENHOEK.	Yes
April 25th 9.20 am	At 9.20 a.m I sent Lieut Phillips and platoon to relieve Lieut Packard at 85th Bde H.Q.	Yes
10 am	At 10 a.m I sent Lieut Burye and platoon to relieve Lt Dalton.	Yes
11.10 am	Lieut Packard and platoon returned.	Yes
1.30 pm	Lieut Dalton and platoon returned. Casualty 1 man wounded, and eight bicycles damaged by Shell fire	Yes

WAR DIARY
or
INTELLIGENCE SUMMARY
(Erase heading not required.)

Army Form C. 2118.

Instructions regarding War Diaries and Intelligence Summaries are contained in F. S. Regs., Part II. and the Staff Manual respectively. Title pages will be prepared in manuscript.

Page 36 Hour, Date, Place	Summary of Events and Information	Remarks and references to Appendices
VLAMERTINGHE April 25th 6pm	I sent Lt. William and platoon to proceed with 11th Inf Brigade to WIELTJE at 6 pm	Ios
April 26th 7.30 am	Lieut Burge and platoon (less Cpl Wilson and 10 men), returned at 7.30 a.m.	Ios.
8 a.m	Lt Dalton and platoon relieved Lieut Phillips at VERLORENHOEK	Ios
8.30 am	I sent Sergt Bumstead and 10 men of No 3 platoon to relieve Cpl Wilcox at St JEAN	Ios
4.30 pm	I sent Lieut Packard and patrol at 4.30 pm to ascertain the result of fighting between BOESINGHE and YPRES. He reported to No 2 28th Division at 9.15 pm.	Ios.
	Lt William and platoon remained with 11th Brigade. Returns were sent up.	Ios

WAR DIARY
or
INTELLIGENCE SUMMARY
(Erase heading not required.)

Army Form C. 2118.

Instructions regarding War Diaries and Intelligence
Summaries are contained in F. S. Regs., Part II.
and the Staff Manual respectively. Title pages
will be prepared in manuscript.

Page 37 Hour, Date, Place	Summary of Events and Information	Remarks and references to Appendices
VLAMERTINGHE		
April 27th 7 am.	Sgt Greenfield and 10 men relieved Sgt Bumstead at Col Sedden HQ at St JEAN. at 7 am	S&S
7.30 am	Lt Phillips and platoon ~~with~~ relieved Lt Dalton and platoon at 85th Bde HQ at 7.30 am	S&S
10.20 am	I sent Lt Packard and patrol to reconnoitre between BOESINGHE and YPRES. He reported to 28th division on return at 2.20 pm	S&S S&S
2.20 pm		
10.30 am	Lt Dalton and platoon returned at 10.30 am	S&S
	I drew one light draught horse from remounts at CAESTRE to complete establishment	S&S
April 28th 7.30 am	I sent Lt Dalton to relieve Lt Phillips and platoon at 85th Bde HQ.	S&S
9.40 am	Sgt Greenfield and party returned at 9.40 am and reported death of Col Sedden.	S&S

WAR DIARY
or
INTELLIGENCE SUMMARY

Army Form C. 2118.

Instructions regarding War Diaries and Intelligence
Summaries are contained in F. S. Regs., Part II.
and the Staff Manual respectively. Title pages
will be prepared in manuscript.

(Erase heading not required.)

Hour, Date, Place	Summary of Events and Information	Remarks and references to Appendices
VLAMERTINGHE		
April 28th		
9.30 am	Lt Phillips and platoon returned at 9.30 am	Yes
2.20 pm	I sent Lt Burge and platoon to relieve the will ? at 11th Bde H.Q. at 2.20 pm	Yes
4.30 pm	Lt William and platoon returned.	Yes
April 29th		
9.30 am	I sent Sergeant Major Lawn to huts ?? of YPRES to ascertain occupants of the camps at 9.30 am	Yes
11.15 am	He returned with report at 11.15 am	Yes
11 pm	I sent Sgt ?? and Mr ?? to guide one battalion 11th Bde from VLAMERTINGHE to VELDHOEK.	Yes

Instructions regarding War Diaries and Intelligence
Summaries are contained in F. S. Regs., Part II.
and the Staff Manual respectively.   Title pages
will be prepared in manuscript.

Page 39

Hour, Date, Place	Summary of Events and Information	Remarks and references to Appendices
VLAMERTINGHE April 30th 3 a.m	Sgt Bunstead returned and reported Battalion had arrived with no casualties	Yes
7.30 am	Lt Packard and platoon left for 11th Bde H.Q.	Yes
8 am	Lt Phillips and platoon left for 85th Bde H.Q To relieve Lt Barge and Lt Dalton	Yes
10.20 am	Lt Barge and Lt Dalton returned	Yes
9.30 am	Lt William and Sgt Bunstead went to reconnoitre roads north and south of POPERINGHE to find a way for transport.	
1.30 pm	Lt William and Sgt Bunstead returned and reported to 28th Division	Yes
	30 - 4 - 15.	Yes

La Lewis Lieut
for Capt
Cmdg 28th Divisional Cyclist Coy.

1247 W 3299 200,000 (E) 8/14 J.B.C. & A. Forms/C. 2118/11.

121/5481

28th Division.

25th Cyclist Coy.

Vol V 1 — 31. 5. 15.

WAR DIARY
or
INTELLIGENCE SUMMARY
(Erase heading not required.)

Army Form C. 2118.

Instructions regarding War Diaries and Intelligence Summaries are contained in F. S. Regs., Part II. and the Staff Manual respectively. Title pages will be prepared in manuscript.

Page 40

Hour, Date, Place	Summary of Events and Information	Remarks and references to Appendices
VLAMERTINGHE May 1st	Nothing to report.	J.a.J.
May 2nd 10.30 am	Lt Williams and platoon proceeded to 11th Brigade Headquarters to relieve Lt Packard.	J.a.J
11 am	Lt Dalton and platoon proceeded to 85th Bde No. 2 to relieve Lt Phillips.	J.a.J
12.15 pm	Lt Packard and platoon returned.	J.a.J
12.45 pm	Lt Phillips and platoon returned. One bicycle and one rifle lost.	J.a.J
May 3rd 5.40 am	L/c Fitzgerald and escort brought in one German prisoner. I sent him to H.Q. 28th Division	J.a.J.
8.30 pm	Lieuts Packard Burge and Phillips left to Guide Cavalry to VELORENHOEK.	J.a.J
May 4th 3.30 am	Lt Dalton and platoon returned. Casualty:- one man killed.	J.a.J.
5. am	Lieuts Packard, Burge and Phillips returned.	J.a.J
6.30 am	Lieut Williams and platoon returned	J.a.J

1247 W 3299 200,000 (E) 8/14 J.B.C. & A. Forms/C. 2118/11.

Instructions regarding War Diaries and Intelligence
Summaries are contained in F. S. Regs., Part II.
and the Staff Manual respectively. Title pages
will be prepared in manuscript.

Page 41

Hour, Date, Place	Summary of Events and Information	Remarks and references to Appendices
VLAMERTINGHE.		
May 5th		
9.30a	The Company moved the Chateau at VLAMERTINGHE to farm	da.
	⊔ H.7.b -	
1-	No 2 Platoon under Lt Burge sent to act as Standing Patrol with the Regiments at rest ⊔ H.5.a ⊔ order to keep touch with Divisional Hd Qrs.	da
2.30p	No 1 Platoon under Lt Packard were employed in burying telephone cables — returned at 6.30p —	da
6.20p	Patrol under Sergt Bumstead sent to report on road at Canal head ⊔ I 2. C.	da
May 6th		
9p.m.	No 6 Platoon under Lieut Phillips relieved No 2 Platoon as Standing Patrol at the huts ⊔ H 5.a – the patrol was then reduced to one N.CO + 6 men.	da
9a -	Sergt Bumstead + 12 men No 3 Platoon employed burying telephone wire —	da

1247   W 3299   200,000   (E) 8/14   J.B.C. & A.   Forms/C. 2118/11.

Instructions regarding War Diaries and Intelligence
Summaries are contained in F. S. Regs., Part II.
and the Staff Manual respectively.   Title pages
will be prepared in manuscript.

Page 42

Hour, Date, Place	Summary of Events and Information	Remarks and references to Appendices
1915. VLAMERTINGHE May 7° 9a.	A standing patrol of 1 NCO & 6 men. No 4 Platoon relieved the standing patrol at Hut Camp —	9a
9a.	Sergt Bumstead & 12 men No 3 Platoon employed burying telephone wire	N.
May 8th 9a.	A standing patrol of 1 N.CO. & 6 men No 5 Platoon relieved No 4 Platoon at Hut Camp —	9a
6 p.m.	An officers Patrol. No 1 Platoon under Lieut Packard was sent to report on position of affairs at POTYZE. A Counter attack was being made by 85th Brigade — The patrol returned at 11.55 p. —	9a
May 9th 9a.	A standing patrol of 1 N.CO 6 men No 1 Platoon relieved No 5 Platoon at Hut Camp —	9a
10 am	Three Patrols under N.C.O; posted in vicinity of VLAMERTINGHE to collect stragglers —	9a

1247 W 3299 200,000 (E) 8/14 J.B.C. & A.   Forms/C. 2118/II.

WAR DIARY
or
INTELLIGENCE SUMMARY
(Erase heading not required.)

Army Form C. 2118.

Instructions regarding War Diaries and Intelligence
Summaries are contained in F. S. Regs., Part II.
and the Staff Manual respectively.   Title pages
will be prepared in manuscript.

Page 43

Hour, Date, Place	Summary of Events and Information	Remarks and references to Appendices
YLAMERTINGHE 1915		
May 10 — 9 a.m.	A patrol of No 1 Platoon relieved No 1 Platoon at Hut Camp.	
9 a.m.	Patrols to collect stragglers found by No 4 Platoon	✓a
	36 Stragglers of various divisions collected & distributed.	✓a
May 11 — 9 a.m.	A Patrol of No 4 Platoon relieved No 6 at Hut Camp.	✓a
	A Patrol of No 5 Platoon collecting stragglers	✓a
	Lieut Jervois struck off the strength of the company on reforming 1st Bn. K.O.Y.L.I.	✓a
12 noon	Patrol of 6 men No 4 Platoon detailed to patrol telephone wires BRANDHOEK – YPRES.	✓a
8 p.m.	A party of 18 men detailed to clear road of dikes at POTYZE.	✓a
8 p.m.	A party under Lieut Phillip detailed to collect arms & equipment in vicinity of trenches.	✓a
	The wagons failed to turn up for this party, so arms were not collected —	✓a

Instructions regarding War Diaries and Intelligence Summaries are contained in F. S. Regs., Part II. and the Staff Manual respectively. Title pages will be prepared in manuscript.

Page 44

Hour, Date, Place	Summary of Events and Information	Remarks and references to Appendices
VLAMERTINGHE 1915		
May 12 -	4a - Wire patrol for 6 hrs. found by No. 2. Platoon -	9a
	9a - Standing patrol at hut Camp. withdrawn	9a
	5.30p - No 2 & 3 Platoon under Lt Burge collected & put arms ammunition & equipment NE & E. of YPRES.	9a
	7.30p - Lt Williams & Dalton with reconnoitring patrol reconnoitred supporting points rear of trenches E. of YRES	9a
May - 13	- No Patrols -	
May - 14	8am - Company left billets at VLAMERTINGHE for WATOU. for rest -	9a
WATOU	11a - Arrived at WATOU. Billetted in farms	9a
May 15	11.30am - Captain F. J. Agg proceeded to take over Brigade Major of 84th Inf. Bde.	MB
	12 noon - Received orders to be prepared to move the company to hold the supporting line of trenches	MB

Instructions regarding War Diaries and Intelligence
Summaries are contained in F. S. Regs., Part II.
and the Staff Manual respectively.   Title pages
will be prepared in manuscript.

Page 45

Hour, Date, Place	Summary of Events and Information	Remarks and references to Appendices
WATOU 1915.		
May 15th 4 pm	The above order cancelled but were warned that we might be required to find working party of 100 for digging trenches under 3rd Cav. Div:	MP
May 16th	No working parties were required.	MP
May 17th 3.30 pm	Received orders to move unit to report to Hqrs 3rd Cav Div: at RENINGHELST via POPERINGHE by whom we should be billeted.	MP
4.45 pm	Moved from WATOU in accordance with above order	MP
7.30 pm	Found billets for the night on POPERINGHE—RENINGHELST road, having joined up with "B" Squadron Surrey Yeomanry	MP
BRANDHOEK May 18th 9 am	Made search for billets in neighbourhood of BRANDHOEK and reported our new billets to 3rd Cav. Div: Hd qrs at	MP
11.30 am	RENINGHELST.	MP
2 pm	Moved to new billet 1 mile West of BRANDHOEK	MP
7.30 pm	Sent out working party of 2 officers — Lieut Buggs and	MP

Instructions regarding War Diaries and Intelligence
Summaries are contained in F. S. Regs., Part II.
and the Staff Manual respectively.   Title pages
will be prepared in manuscript.

Page 46

Hour, Date, Place	Summary of Events and Information	Remarks and references to Appendices
BRANDHOEK May 18th 1915	Lieut. Phillips and 102 NCO's + men to report to 27th Div. R.E. for digging + improving trenches near the Level crossing on YPRES - MENIN road.	ww
May 19th 3.30am	This party returned to billets.	ww
May 20th 7.0pm	Sent working party of 2 officers. Lieut Williams + Lieut Dalton and 102 N.C.O's + men as on 18th inst.	
7.30pm	Capt. Agg returned to take over Command.	
8. pm	2nd Lieut. Hawkins, 3rd Bn. S. Staffs Regt joined for duty.	ww
May 21st 3.30 am	Above working party returned.	
6. pm	Lieut Packard + 2nd Lieut Hawkins took a patrol of 4 NCO's + 12 men to watch bridges No's 7 to 14 over canal from N.W. to S.W. of YPRES.	
9 pm	Lieut Packard returned.	
11.30 pm	2nd Lieut Hawkins returned.	ww
May 22nd 9. am	Patrols on bridges No's 7 to 14 relieved and reduced to 1 N.C.O. and 3 men.	ww

Instructions regarding War Diaries and Intelligence
Summaries are contained in F. S. Regs., Part II.
and the Staff Manual respectively.   Title pages
will be prepared in manuscript.

Hour, Date, Place	Summary of Events and Information	Remarks and references to Appendices
Page 4? BRANDHOEK		
May 22nd 1915 5.30pm	Moved company into billets in farm 1500 yds. W. of VLAMERTINGHE	MP
May 23rd 2.30pm	Lieut Burge & Lieut Hawkins with No 2 Platoon proceeded to YPRES in search of Equipment, rifles & ammunition	MP
6.pm	Above party returned.	
May 24th 6.45am	Received orders to send patrols to the front to report on situation	
7.15am	Lieut Williams & No 4 Platoon left billets.	
7.30am	Moved company to farm on South side of YPRES - VLAMERTINGHE road 300 yds E. of level crossing	
8 am.	Sent patrol of 1 N.C.O. and 3 men to remain on main road to collect stragglers and bring them to farm	
8.30am.	Lieut. Packard & patrol of 1 N.C.O. & 3 men visited bridges 7 to 14 found all correct & relieved the previous day's patrol.	
9 am.	Lieut Packard returned.	
9.15am	Capt. Agg ordered to report to 86th Inf Bde. Lieut Packard took over temporary command	
11.30am	2 Lieut Dalton and patrol of 1 N.C.O. & 3 men sent to discover the position of Lieut. Williams & his platoon.	MP

1247 W 3299 200,000 (E) 8/14 J.B.C. & A.   Forms/C. 2118/11.

WAR DIARY
or
INTELLIGENCE SUMMARY *nd.*

(Erase heading not required.)

Army Form C. 2118.

Instructions regarding War Diaries and Intelligence
Summaries are contained in F. S. Regs., Part II.
and the Staff Manual respectively.   Title pages
will be prepared in manuscript.

Hour, Date, Place		Summary of Events and Information	Remarks and references to Appendices
Page 4d.	BRANDHOEK		
	1915.		
May 24th	11.30 am	Capt. Agg returned to command	
	2.15 pm	Message received from Lieut Williams explaining present situation and his position — dug outs near white château of POTIJZE	
	7.30 pm	2 Lieut. Dalton returned	
	7 pm	Stragglers of all regiments handed over to Transport Officers going up with rations to their Bde Hqrs.	
May 25th	12.30 am	In all 159 stragglers were collected up till midnight 24/25 Returned with Company to billets W. of VLAMERTINGHE.	
	9.0 am	66 stragglers collected by patrol during the night, and brought back to billet and sent on to Transport lines 1 Patrol of 1 N.C.O. and 3 men sent to relieve bridge patrol of previous day.	nd.
	8 pm	2 Lieut. Dalton posted guards on bridges Nos. 7 to 11 inclusive Each guard 1 N.C.O. and 3 men. (No 2nd 5 Platoon). Above patrol relieved.	
	11.30 pm	2 Lieut. Dalton & his platoon Sergeant returned	nd
May 26th	10.30 am	Above guards relieved by No 6 platoon.	
	4 pm	Lieut Burge & Lieut. Hawkins with 50 men of Nos 2 + 3 Platoon	

Instructions regarding War Diaries and Intelligence Summaries are contained in F. S. Regs., Part II. and the Staff Manual respectively.   Title pages will be prepared in manuscript.

Page 49

Hour, Date, Place	Summary of Events and Information	Remarks and references to Appendices
BRANDHOEK		
May 26ᵗʰ 1915.	proceeded to bridge No 14 over canal S.W. of YPRES to carry 'Knife rests' from there to the PORTE DE LILLE	
3.30 a.m.	This party returned — one Lance-Sergeant wounded.	
	Lieut Phillips visited the bridge guards during the night and reported that two French soldiers were apprehended for looting & handed over to the Military police — also 2 civilians without passes.	
May 27ᵗʰ 10 a.m.	Bridge guards relieved by No 1 Platoon.	
12 noon	Guards visited by Lieut Packard & platoon sergeant.	
4.31 pm	Two guides were provided to 85 Bde. Hqrs. for 9ᵗʰ Bde. Guides for two companies — four men — & proceed via No 13 bridge to PORTE DE LILLE — Also two guides for transport of Suffolk Rgt. up to Halt. Also two N.C.O.'s to guide officers of 9ᵗʰ Bde. to POTIJZE. All guides found from No 4 Platoon.	
May 28ᵗʰ 10 a.m.	Bridge guards relieved by No 5 Platoon.	
11.30 a.m.	Guards visited by Lieut. Dalton & platoon sergeant.	
	Guides as for the previous night —	
May 29ᵗʰ 10.0	Bridge guards relieved by No 6 Platoon	
	visited by Lieut Phillips —	

Instructions regarding War Diaries and Intelligence
Summaries are contained in F. S. Regs., Part II.
and the Staff Manual respectively.   Title pages
will be prepared in manuscript.

Page 5⁰⁴

Hour, Date, Place	Summary of Events and Information	Remarks and references to Appendices
1915		
May 30ᵗʰ.	Orders received 12.5 a.. to move to rest area at WATOU thr day —	
9.30 a.	Company left BRANDHOEK.	
11 a —	Company arrived WATOU – Billetted in farms. K. 8 d. & K. 9 c.	da
WATOU	Platoon – rest area placed at disposal of platoon officers —	da
May 31ˢᵗ.		

1 June – 1915.

E. J. J. Aylet Capt.
Cdg 28 Divisional Cyclist Company

1247   W 3299   200,000   (E)   8/14   J.B.C. & A.   Forms/C. 2118/11.

28th Division   187/587/5

25th Cyclist Coy.
_____
Vol VI 1 — 30.6.15.

Instructions regarding War Diaries and Intelligence
Summaries are contained in F. S. Regs., Part II.
and the Staff Manual respectively. Title pages
will be prepared in manuscript.

Page 51

Hour, Date, Place	Summary of Events and Information	Remarks and references to Appendices
WATOU		
June 1st 1915	The Company in rest area – nothing to report.	ub.
2nd	Nothing to report. 20 men proceeded on furlough –	
3rd 5.30 pm	Moved to new billets in farm in K9d.	ub.
4	Nothing to report.	ub.
5	" "	ub
6	Sunday – Company at rest –	
7	20 men returned from furlough	ub.
	Platoons at disposal of Platoon Commanders	ub
8	20 men proceeded on furlough	
	Platoons placed at disposal of Platoon Commanders	ub

1247 W 3299 200,000 (E) 8/14 J.B.C. & A.   Forms/C. 2118/11.

Instructions regarding War Diaries and Intelligence
Summaries are contained in F. S. Regs., Part II.
and the Staff Manual respectively.   Title pages
will be prepared in manuscript.

(Erase heading not required.)

Hour, Date, Place	Summary of Events and Information	Remarks and references to Appendices
WATOU 1915 June 9ᵗʰ	8 a.m. Route march & Tactical Exercise in vicinity of WINNIZEELE. 4.30 p.m. Company sent out in patrols to practice Road reconnaissance	ℳ
June 10ᵗ	Capt. Clegg joined 84ᵗʰ Brigade temporarily as staff Captain. Tactical operations in conjunction with Surrey Yeomanry	
June 11ᵗ	Company at disposal of Platoon officers	ℳ
June 12	Company at musketry at CASSEL.	ℳ
June 13	Church parade	ℳ
June 14	Company moved to WESTOUTRE with Divisional H. Qrs. The Company marched via ABEELE - BOESCHEPE - WESTOUTRE	ℳ

Pay 67

1247 W 3299 200,000 (E) 8/14 J.B.C. & A.   Forms/C. 2118/11.

WAR DIARY
or
INTELLIGENCE SUMMARY

(Erase heading not required.)

Army Form C. 2118.

Instructions regarding War Diaries and Intelligence
Summaries are contained in F. S. Regs., Part II.
and the Staff Manual respectively. Title pages
will be prepared in manuscript.

Hour, Date, Place	Summary of Events and Information	Remarks and references to Appendices
Page 5·3 WESTOUTRE.		
June 14th . 5.30p.	Company arrived at WESTOUTRE + billetted at M 20.a	
June - 15th -	Company patrolled the country in vicinity of LOCRE, LA CLYTTE + DICKEBUSH -	
June - 16 -	Company patrolled country in vicinity, making themselves acquainted with all roads -	
June - 17th	Platoon at disposal of platoon Commander - Special instruction to N.C.O -	
" 18th	Lieut J. A Daniel - The Welch Regt. joined the company for duty, and took over command of No 1 Platoon from Lieut Packard.	
3 o p.m.	Lieut Dalton + platoon went to DICKEBUSCH to patrol roads and communication wires in the district E. of LA CLYTTE- DICKEBUSCH road.	

Instructions regarding War Diaries and Intelligence Summaries are contained in F. S. Regs., Part II. and the Staff Manual respectively. Title pages will be prepared in manuscript.

(Erase heading not required.)

Hour, Date, Place	Summary of Events and Information	Remarks and references to Appendices
Page 54 WESTOUTRE 1915. June 19ᵗʰ	Nos. 1, 2, 3 and 4 Platoons placed at disposal of platoon commanders.	
3.0 pm	Lieut Phillips and platoon went to Relieve No 5 platoon	Mr
5.0 pm	Lieut Dalton returned	
20ᵗʰ 10.30am	Church parade.	
3.0 pm	Lieut Daniel & platoon relieved No 6 who returned at 4.30 pm	Mr.
21ˢᵗ	Platoons 2, 3, 4, and 5, and 6 at disposal of platoon commanders	
3.0 pm	Lieut Burge & platoon relieved No 1, who returned at 5 pm	Mr
22ⁿᵈ 10 am	Lieut Packard went to DICKEBUSCH to visit patrols	
4.0 pm	Lieut Hawkins & platoon relieved No 2, who returned to billets at 5.30 pm.	Mr.
23ʳᵈ 10 am	Nos 1, 2, 5, & 6 Platoons went for route march & tactical exercise in the vicinity of ST JANS CAPELLE, under O.C. Company.	Mr.
3.0 pm	Lieut Williams & platoon relieved No. 3, who returned at 5 pm	Mr.

1247 W 3299 200,000 (E) 8/14 J.B.C. & A. Forms/C. 2118/11.

Instructions regarding War Diaries and Intelligence Summaries are contained in F. S. Regs., Part II. and the Staff Manual respectively. Title pages will be prepared in manuscript.

Page 55 Hour, Date, Place	Summary of Events and Information	Remarks and references to Appendices
WESTOUTRE. 1915	No 1, 2, 3, and 6 Platoons at disposal of platoon commanders	
June 24th 3.0 pm	Lieut Dalton's platoon relieved No 4 who returned to billets about 5.30 pm	und
25th	Nos. 1, 2, 3 and 4 platoons went for tactical exercise in the vicinity of BERTHEN under O.C. Company	
3.0 pm	Lieut. Phillips relieved No 5 who returned at 5.30 pm	und
26th	Platoons Nos. 2, 3, 4 and 5 placed at disposal of platoon commanders.	
3.0 pm	Lieut Daniel's platoon relieved No 6, who returned to billets at 4.30 pm	und
	A fatigue of one platoon No 7 provided to clear the stream running from slopes of MONT NOIR into WESTOUTRE.	
27th 11. am	Church parade. No. 3	
	Fatigue party of one platoon, as above from 8 - 12.30 and 2 - 6.30.	
3.0 pm	Lieut Guys relieved No 1 platoon. They returned to billets 5.30 pm.	und

1247   W 3299   200,000   (E) 8/14   J.B.C. & A.   Forms/C. 2118/11.

Instructions regarding War Diaries and Intelligence
Summaries are contained in F. S. Regs., Part II.
and the Staff Manual respectively. Title pages
will be prepared in manuscript.

Hour, Date, Place	Summary of Events and Information	Remarks and references to Appendices
1915 WESTOUTRE		
June 28th	Nos 1, 2, 5, and 6 platoons at disposal of platoon commanders.	
8.30-12 noon	No 4. Platoon on fatigue clearing stream.	
3.0 pm	No 3 Platoon, Lieut Hawkins - relieved No 2. who returned to billets at 6.0 pm	MW.
June 29th 9.30 am	Capt. Agg and Lieut. Packard gave instruction to six N.C.O.s in the neighbourhood of DUDERDOM - DICKEBUSCH. and at	
11.0 am	visited Lieut Hawkins and his patrols.	
3.0 pm	Lieut Williams : No 4 Platoon relieved No 3, who returned to billets at 5.30 pm	MW.
June 30th 9.30 - 12 noon	Two platoons Nos 1 and 6 completed work of clearing stream	
3.0 pm	Lieut. Dalton No 5 Platoon relieved No. 4 at DICKEBUSCH the latter returning to billets at 5.15 pm.	MW.

J J Agg Capt.

1-7-15.   Cdg 2/8 D of L Regt Bn.

28th Division

181/6314

28th Cyclist Coy.

Vol VII 1 — 31. 7. 15.

WAR DIARY
or
INTELLIGENCE SUMMARY

(Erase heading not required.)

Army Form C. 2118.

Instructions regarding War Diaries and Intelligence
Summaries are contained in F. S. Regs., Part II.
and the Staff Manual respectively. Title pages
will be prepared in manuscript.

28th CYCLIST COMPANY
Date: July & 31 July

Hour, Date, Place	Summary of Events and Information	Remarks and references to Appendices
Page 57 WESTOUTRE		
July 1st 1915. 9am	Capt. Agg & Lieut. Packard proceeded to SCHERPENBERG to post a standing patrol of 2 NCO's and 6 men of No. 3 Platoon. then visited patrols in neighbourhood of VIERSTRAAT.	
3 p.m.	No 6 Platoon relieved No 5 at DICKEBUSCH	MS
6 pm	No 5 Platoon returned to billets.	
July 2nd 10 am	O.C. Cy lectured in billets.	
10 am	No 1 Platoon relieved No 6 at DICKEBUSCH	MS.
3 pm	No 6 Platoon returned.	
5.45 pm	Capt. Agg & Lieut. Packard visited patrol at SCHERPENBERG also instructed 6 NCOs in map reading en route.	
July 3rd 9.30 am		
3 pm	No 2 Platoon relieved No 1 at DICKEBUSCH.	
6 pm	No 1 Platoon returned to billets.	
7 pm	Nos. 4 and 6 platoons - Lieuts Williams & Phillips proceeded to DICKEBUSCH to report to R.E. for digging in cable lines towards the trenches.	MS
July 4th 3.30 am	Above platoons returned to billets.	
8.15 am	No 1 Platoon proceeded to neighbourhood of KEMMEL	

1247 W 3299 200,000 (E) 8/14 J.B.C. & A.   Forms/C. 2118/11.

Instructions regarding War Diaries and Intelligence Summaries are contained in F. S. Regs., Part II. and the Staff Manual respectively. Title pages will be prepared in manuscript.

Hour, Date, Place		Summary of Events and Information	Remarks and references to Appendices
Page 60 WESTOUTRE	1915.		
July 9th	3.30 am	Trench digging party & cable party returned to billets.	
	8.30 am	No 6 platoon went to KEMMEL for digging in wires.	
	3.30 p.	2 N.C.O's + 4 men of No 5 platoon relieved patrol of No 1 at DICKEBUSCH who returned at 5.30 pm.	
	6 pm	No 6 platoon returned having completed the work at KEMMEL	
	7.30 pm	No's 3 & 4 platoons proceeded to DICKEBUSCH for digging in cable wires	M.S.
July 10th	3.30 am	Above party returned.	
	3.30 pm M.S.	2 NCO's + 4 men of No 6 Platoon relieved patrol of No 5 at DICKEBUSCH, who returned at 1.30 pm. M.S.	
	12 noon		
	7 pm	50 men of Nos 1 and 2 platoons under Lieut Bucye & Lieut Daniel proceeded to draw tools at DICKEBUSCH — marched to cross roads 500 yds W.N.W. of VIERSTRAAT and dug a subsidiary line of trenches S.W. of VIERSTRAAT.	M.S.
July 11th	3.45 am	Above party returned.	
	11 am	Church parade.	
	12 noon	2 N.C.O's and 4 men of No 1 Platoon relieved patrol of No 6 at DICKEBUSCH who returned at 1.30 pm	
	7 pm	50 men of Nos. 3 & 4 platoons under Lieut Williams &	M.S.

1247 W 3299 200,000 (E) 8/14 J.D.C. & A. Forms/C. 2118/11.

WAR DIARY
or
INTELLIGENCE SUMMARY *pub.*

Army Form C. 2118.

Instructions regarding War Diaries and Intelligence
Summaries are contained in F. S. Regs., Part II.
and the Staff Manual respectively. Title pages
will be prepared in manuscript.

(Erase heading not required.)

Hour, Date, Place	Summary of Events and Information	Remarks and references to Appendices
Page 61. WESTOUTRE. 1915. July 11th (continued)	Lieut. Hawkins proceeded to dig the subsidiary line of trenches as on previous night in neighbourhood of VIERSTRAAT.	M.O.
July 12th 3.45 a.m. 9.30 a.m.	Above party returned to billets. 2 N.C.O's and 4 men of No 2 platoon relieved patrol of No XI at DICKEBUSCH.	
1.0 pm 8 p.m.	Lieut Phillip & Lieut Daniel sent to report to C.R.E. at DICKEBUSCH to view work to be done on trenches. 50 men of Nos 5 & 6 platoons under Lieut Philish & Lieut Dalton proceeded to VIERSTRAAT to dig as on previous night.	M.O.
July 13th 3 a.m. 9.30 a.m.	Above party returned. 2 N.C.O's & 4 men of No 3 platoon relieved patrol of No 2 at DICKEBUSCH.	
8 pm	50 men of Nos 1 and 2 platoons under Lieut Daniel & Burge proceeded to VIERSTRAAT to dig trenches.	M.O.
July 14th 3 a.m. 12 noon	Above party returned. 2 N.C.O's & 4 men of N. 4. platoon went on patrol to DICKEBUSCH to relieve No 3.	
8 pm	50 men from Nos 3 & 4 platoons under Lieut Williams & Lieut Hawkins went to VIERSTRAAT to dig trenches of subsidiary line	
12 midnight	Above party returned — unable to dig owing to heavy rain	M.O.

WAR DIARY
or
INTELLIGENCE SUMMARY
(Erase heading not required.)

Army Form C. 2118.

Instructions regarding War Diaries and Intelligence
Summaries are contained in F. S. Regs., Part II.
and the Staff Manual respectively.   Title pages
will be prepared in manuscript.

Page 62

Hour, Date, Place	Summary of Events and Information	Remarks and references to Appendices
WESTOUTRE.		
July 15th	1915 9am to 8pm. 1 N.C.O. 16 men lent to O.C. Signal Coy. for laying wires.	
	12 noon Patrol at DICKEBUSCH withdrawn, being no longer in divisional area.	
	2 pm. Patrols from Nos 1 + 2 platoons visited KEMMEL - LOCRE - DRANOUTRE area - for purpose of reconnoitring roads. Lieut. Packard also visited same area.	
	8 pm. Digging party of 50 men - (Nos 5 + 6 platoons) under Lieut. Phillips + Lieut. Dalton proceeded to VIERSTRAAT.	M.R.
July 16th	3 am. Above party returned	
	9 am to 8pm 1 N.C.O. + 6 men lent to O.C. Signal Coy. as previous day.	
	2 pm. Patrols from Nos 3 + 4 visited KEMMEL - LOCRE - DRANOUTRE area. Lieut. Packard visited SCHERPENBERG.	
	8 pm. Digging party of 50 men - (Nos 1 + 2 platoons) under Lieut. Daniel proceeded via KEMMEL to neighbourhood of SANDBAG VILLA to dig subsidiary line of trenches.	M.R.
July 17th	3 am. Above party returned	
	1 p.m. Capt. Agg + Lieut. Packard went to 84th Inf Bde Hqrs at KEMMEL and reconnoitred neighbourhood of MONT KEMMEL to arrange for guards + police posts for hill	
	8 pm. Digging party of 50 men as previous night. (Nos 3 + 4 platoons) under Lieut. Phillips + Lieut. Hawkins.	M.R.

1247   W 3299   200,000 (E) 8/14   J.B.C. & A.   Forms/C. 2118/11.

Instructions regarding War Diaries and Intelligence Summaries are contained in F. S. Regs., Part II. and the Staff Manual respectively. Title pages will be prepared in manuscript.

Hour, Date, Place	Summary of Events and Information	Remarks and references to Appendices
Page 63 WESTOUTRE		
July 18th 1915 2.30 am	Digging party returned	
	1 N.C.O. 16 men sent to O.C. Signal Coy for cable work	
8 am - 4 pm	Church parade	
11 am		
8 pm	Digging party Nos 4 & 6 platoons (Lieut. Williams + 2nd Lieut. Dalton) proceeded to SANDBAG VILLA as usual, to dig subsidiary line.	M.R.
July 19th 2.30 am	Above party returned	
	1 N.C.O. + 10 men led to O.C. Signal Coy for cable work.	
8 am - 4 pm	All officers employed in searching a large area in neighbourhood	
9 am - 4 pm	of BOESCHEPE - Mt. DES CATS - BERTHEN - SCHAEXKEN - MT NOIR - WESTOUTRE for billets, in accordance with orders from 28th Div.	
8 pm	Digging party Nos 6 + 1 platoons (Lieut. Phillips + Lieut. Daniel) proceeded to same locality. (No 5 Platoon)	M.R.
9 am	Sergt. Trim + 23 other ranks took over guard at Div. H.q.⁴ at WESTOUTRE	
July 20th 3 am	Digging party returned	
	1 N.C.O. + 10 men led to O.C. Signals for cable work.	
8 am - 4 pm	Lieut. Packard + Lieut. Hawkins went to KEMMEL to report to R.E. to look over work to be done on trenches for next 4 days	
2.30 pm		
8 pm	Digging party - Nos 1 + 2 platoons (Lieut. Packard + Lieut. Daniel) proceeded to subsidiary line as usual. Capt. Agg also inspected the work. M.R.	

1247 W 3299 200,000 (E) 8/14 J.B.C. & A. Forms/C. 2118/11.

Instructions regarding War Diaries and Intelligence
Summaries are contained in F. S. Regs., Part II.
and the Staff Manual respectively. Title pages
will be prepared in manuscript.

Hour, Date, Place		Summary of Events and Information	Remarks and references to Appendices
WESTOUTRE.	1915		
July 21st	2.30 am	Digging party returned.	
	8 pm	Digging party Nos. 2 & 3 platoons under Lieut Williams & 2 Lieut Hawkins proceeded to usual locality	MD.
	~~2.30 am~~	~~Digging party returned~~ MD.	
	9.30 pm	A party of 22 N.C.O.'s & men rejoined from ROUEN base	
July 22nd	2.30 am	Digging party returned.	
	10 am	N.C.O.'s from Nos. 1 · 4 · & 6 platoons went under platoon officers to learn positions of battalion & brigade headquarters in neighbourhood of KEMMEL and WULVERGHEM.	MD.
		Digging party no longer required	MD.
July 23rd	10.30 am	Lieut. Pollard visited SCHERPENBERG guard	MD.
July 24th	8 am	½ Sergt. and 20 men - Nos platoon - sent on fatigue to neighbourhood of CROIX-de-POPERINGHE to clean horses.	MD.
July 25th		Nothing to report.	
July 26th	8.15 am	Nos. 2 · 3 · and 4 platoons under Lieut Bugg & Lieut Hawkins went to 6 pm to dig in cable wires about ½ mile W. of KEMMEL.	MD.
	8 pm	Nos. 1 & 6 platoon under Lieut. Daniel proceeded to same locality but in a more exposed position for same work	MD.

1247 W 3299 200,000 (E) 8/14 J.B.C. & A.   Forms/C. 2118/11.

Instructions regarding War Diaries and Intelligence Summaries are contained in F. S. Regs., Part II. and the Staff Manual respectively. Title pages will be prepared in manuscript.

(Erase heading not required.)

Hour, Date, Place	Summary of Events and Information	Remarks and references to Appendices
Page 65 WESTOUTRE. 1915		
July 26th (cont'd) 11 am	Capt. Hopp visited SCHERPENBERG. Cable digging party returned to billets.	MP.
" 27th 3 am	Nos. 2, 3, & 4 Platoons under Lieut Williams & 2nd Lieut Hawkins	
8 am	proceeded to same locality returned 5.30 p.m. Nos. 1 and 6 Platoons under Lieut Daniel, and 2nd Lieut Dalton	MP8
" 28th 8 am	proceeded to neighbourhood of KEMMEL to dig in cable wires.	
4.30 pm	Above party returned. Nos 4 and 6 platoons under Lieut. Williams & Lieut Phillips	MP
" 29th 8 am	proceeded to same locality to lay cable line. Lieut Packard visited SCHERPENBERG.	
5 pm	Digging party returned.	MP
6 pm	No 1 Platoon under Lieut. Daniel proceeded to same locality	
" 30th 8 am	& completed work of digging in wires there. Returned 4 pm. Received orders for an officer to visit the guards over wells in MONT NOIR by day & night. Duty performed by an officer detailed weekly.	MP

WAR DIARY
or
INTELLIGENCE SUMMARY *n.d.*
(Erase heading not required.)

Army Form C. 2118.

Instructions regarding War Diaries and Intelligence
Summaries are contained in F. S. Regs., Part II.
and the Staff Manual respectively. Title pages
will be prepared in manuscript.

Page 66

Hour, Date, Place	Summary of Events and Information	Remarks and references to Appendices
WESTOUTRE July 31st 1915 8.15 am	Nos 2 - 3 - + 4 platoons under Lieut. Burge + Lieut Hawkins proceeded to cross roads ½ mi S.W of LINDENHOEK to dig in cable line from there to 85th Bde Hqs. on KEMMEL - NEUVE EGLISE road - returned 5.30 p.m. Aug 1st 1915.	n.d.

[signature] Capt
Cdg 28 Dv [?] Coy

28th Division

121 / 6650

28th Cyclist Coy

Vol VIII

From 1 - 31. 8. 15

Instructions regarding War Diaries and Intelligence
Summaries are contained in F. S. Regs., Part II.
and the Staff Manual respectively. Title pages
will be prepared in manuscript.

WAR DIARY
or
INTELLIGENCE SUMMARY 2nd
(Erase heading not required.)

Army Form C. 2118.

28th CYCLIST COMPANY
Date 1-8-15 to 31-8-15

Hour, Date, Place	Summary of Events and Information	Remarks and references to Appendices
Page 67. WESTOUTRE.		
August 1st 1915. 8am	Nos. 3, 4, and 6 platoons under Lieut. Williams & Lieut. Phillips went to neighbourhood of LINDENHOEK for digging in cable lines.	
5.30 pm	Above party returned	N.d.
August 2nd 8 am	Nos 1, 2, and 6 platoons under Lieut Burge & Lieut Daniel went to same neighbourhood for digging in cable wires	
11 am	Capt. Agg, Lieut Packard visited the working party and also 85th Bde Hqt.	
3 pm	A reinforcement of 2 men arrived from ROUEN.	N.d.
5.15 pm	Digging party returned	
August 3rd 8 am	Nos. 2, 3, and 4 platoons under Lieut. Williams & 2nd Lieut Hawkins proceeded to same neighbourhood for digging in wires.	N.d.
5.15 pm	Above party returned	
August 4th 8 am	Nos 1, 4, and 6 platoons under Lieut Daniel & Lieut Phillips went to same neighbourhood for digging in cable lines.	N.d.
5.30 pm	Above party returned	
	Lieut. Burge reported to Hqr R.F.C. at St OMER with view to transfer.	
August 5th 8 am	Nos. 1, 2 and 3 platoons under Lieut. Burge & 2nd Lieut Hawkins went to same neighbourhood for digging in cables. Completed the work and returned to billet 4.30 pm	N.d.

WAR DIARY
or
INTELLIGENCE SUMMARY

(Erase heading not required.)

Instructions regarding War Diaries and Intelligence Summaries are contained in F. S. Regs., Part II. and the Staff Manual respectively. Title pages will be prepared in manuscript.

Page 68

Hour, Date, Place	Summary of Events and Information	Remarks and references to Appendices
WESTOUTRE 1915		
August 6th 8.15 am	Nos. 3, 4, and 6 platoons under Lieut. Williams & Lieut Philipps proceeded to dig in cable lines in the neighbourhood of BRULOOZE – Returned at 5. pm	MP
August 7th 8.15 am	Nos. 1, 2 and 6 platoons under Lieut Buege & Lieut Daniel went to dig in wires in same locality as previous day. Completed the work & returned to billets.	MP
4 pm	Lieuts Packard, Williams, Daniel, Philipps, & 2/Lieuts Hawkins	
August 8th 8.30 am	& Dalton & 8 NCO's went to waggon line of 62nd Battery RFA near ZEVECOTEN to receive instruction in disabling guns etc. 1 N.C.O & 6 men lent to O.C. Signal Coy. for duty.	MP
9 am.	Nothing to report	MP
August 9th		
August 10th 8.15 am	Nos 2 and 3 platoons under 2/Lieut Hawkins proceeded to neighbourhood of BUS FARM. 85th 14th Bde Hqs to dig in cables thence to 84th Inf Bde Hqs at KEMMEL CHATEAU. returned 5 p.m.	
10.30 am	2 men detailed to report to Lieut Woodhall – Surrey Yeomanry for salvage work – tobe temporarily attached to him Lieut Packard visited O.C. 37th Div Cyclists at CAESTRE to arrange for instruction of officers, ncos & men of the latter unit.	MP

Instructions regarding War Diaries and Intelligence Summaries are contained in F. S. Regs., Part II. and the Staff Manual respectively. Title pages will be prepared in manuscript.

Hour, Date, Place		Summary of Events and Information	Remarks and references to Appendices
Page 69 WESTOUTRE.	1915.		
August 10th (contd)	7.30 p.m.	Lieut. Williams & No. 4 platoon proceeded to neighbourhood of 84th Inf. Bde. Hqs to dig & improve WULVERGHEM switch trench line under supervision of 38th Fd Coy. R.E.	and
August 11th	2.45 a.m.	Above party returned to billets.	
	8.15 a.m.	Nos. 1 and 6 platoons under Lieut. Philips continued work of digging in cable lines near LINDENHOEK and returned to billets at 4.30 p.m.	and
	7.30 p.m.	Lieut. Bugh & No. 2 platoon continued work on WULVERGHEM switch trench line	
August 12th	8.15 a.m.	Above party returned to billets. Nos. 3 and 4 platoons under Lieut. Hawkins continued work of digging in wires near LINDENHOEK and returned to billets at	
	5.30 p.m. 11 a.m.	Capt. Agg visited SCHERPENBERG	
	3.30 p.m.	2 officers and 30 other ranks of 37th Divisional Cyclist Coy. arrived to be attached for instruction.	
	7.30 p.m.	No. 6 platoon under Lieut. Phillips continued work on WULVERGHEM switch trench line	and
August 13th		Above party returned to billets. Nos. 1 and 2 platoons under Lieut. Daniel continued work of	
	8.15 a.m.	digging in telephone wires near LINDENHOEK returned to billets 4.45 p.m.	

1247 W 3299 200,000 (E) 8/14 J.B.C. & A. Forms/C. 2118/11.

Instructions regarding War Diaries and Intelligence
Summaries are contained in F. S. Regs., Part II.
and the Staff Manual respectively. Title pages
will be prepared in manuscript.

Page 70 Hour, Date, Place 1915	Summary of Events and Information	Remarks and references to Appendices
WESTOUTRE.		
August 13th (cont.) 9.30 a.m to 12.30 p.m	One party of 37th Div. Cyclists under an officer sent out to learn country in neighbourhood of OUDERDOM & RENINGHELST etc. Another party under an officer to neighbourhood of DRANOUTRE - LOCRE.	
6.30 p.m	Digging party of No 3 Platoon with 2 officers + 30 men of 37th Divn Cyclists attached, under Lieut Dalton continued work on WOLVERGHEM switch trench line.	
7.15 p.m.	No 6 Platoon under Lieut. Hawkins continued work of digging in wires between LINDENHOEK and KEMMEL	
9 p.m.	1 Officer + 13 men of 37th Div. Cyclists detached from Lieut. Dalton's party & joined Lieut Hawkins party	(AA)
August 14th 3 a.m.	Lieut Dalton's party returned to billets	
4 a.m.	& Lieut. Hawkins party returned to billets	
8.15 a.m.	No 6 Platoon under Lieut. Philips continued work of digging in cables between LINDENHOEK and KEMMEL returned	5.30 p.m. Capt Agg proceeded to
3 p.m.	Lieut. Packard took detachment of 37th Div Cyclists to MONT ROUGE for instruction	12 noon Divl Hqs - handed over company to Lieut. Packard.
6.30 p.m	Digging party of No 1 Platoon under Lieut Daniel continued the work on WOLVERGHEM switch trench line. No 2 Platoon under Lieut. Burgh completed the work of digging	
7.15 p.m	billets to 11.15 in wires to 84th Bde. battee headquarters.	(AA)

1247 W 3299 200,000 (E) 8/14 J.B.C. & A. Forms/C. 2118/11.

WAR DIARY
or
INTELLIGENCE SUMMARY
(Erase heading not required.)

Army Form C. 2118.

Instructions regarding War Diaries and Intelligence
Summaries are contained in F. S. Regs., Part II.
and the Staff Manual respectively.   Title pages
will be prepared in manuscript.

Hour, Date, Place	Summary of Events and Information	Remarks and references to Appendices
Page 71	1915	
WESTOUTRE 7.30	Lieut. Burgz returned to billets	
August 15th 3 a.m.	Lieut. Daniel returned to billets	
9 a.m. to 1 p.m.	Two parties of 37th Div. Cyclists, under Lieut. Packard & Lieut. Dalton proceeded out to learn the country the former to neighbourhood of OODERDOM - RENINGHELST the - the latter to LOCRE & DRANOUTRE	
7.15 p.m.	No. 3 Platoon under Lieut. Hawkins continued work on WOLVERGHEM switch trench lines.	W.
August 16th 3 a.m.	A box party returned.	
8.30	A party of 37th Div. Cyclists proceeded to neighbourhood of	
12 noon	VLAMERTINGHE - YPRES under an officer	
3 p.m.	Detachment of 37th Div. Cyclists left to rejoin their own unit	
	being replaced by another detachment of equal strength.	
8 p.m.	Lieut. Phillips & 15 NCOs & men of No. 6 Platoon proceeded to 25th Bde Hqs to be shown positions of Bn Headquarters & battn headquarters & methods of approach by day & night.	W.
August 17th 8 a.m.	No. 4 Platoon under Lieut. Daniel continued work on WOLVERGHEM switch trench line. 1 officer & 14 men of the 37th Div Cyclists were attached to this party. The remainder of detachment of 37th Cyclists were sent to DRANOUTRE and LOCRE to learn the country.	

WAR DIARY
or
INTELLIGENCE SUMMARY MP

(Erase heading not required.)

Army Form C. 2118.

Instructions regarding War Diaries and Intelligence
Summaries are contained in F. S. Regs., Part II.
and the Staff Manual respectively.   Title pages
will be prepared in manuscript.

Hour, Date, Place	Summary of Events and Information	Remarks and references to Appendices
WESTOUTRE. 1915		
August 17th (cont) 1 p.m.	Capt. Agg returned to take over command of Coy.	
8 p.m.	Lieut. Burge + 15 N.C.O.'s & men went to 85th Inf Bde to learn approaches to Bn Hq & battee Hqs. Lieut. Hawkins + 15 N.C.O.'s & men went to 84th Inf Bde for same purpose.	MP
August 18th 8 am	No 5 platoon under Lieut. Dalton proceeded MP continued work on WULVERGHEM switch trenches. 1 officer + 14 other ranks of 37th Divl Cyclists were attached to his party for instruction. The remainder of the detachment of 37th Divl Cyclists proceeded to DRANOUTRE + NEUVE ÉGLISE to learn the country.	
4 pm	Digging party returned to billets.	MP
August 19th 8 am	No 6 platoon under Lieut. Phillips continued work on WULVERGHEM switch trenches	
8 p.m.	No 3 platoon (15 men) under Lieut Hawkins reconnoitred Bn HdQrs of 83 Brigade	
	No 4 platoon (15 men) under Lieut Oskwith Williams reconnoitred Bn HdQrs. of 84th Brigade	
	No 5 platoon (15 men) under Lieut Dalton reconnoitred Bn Hd Qrs of 85 Brigade	

Instructions regarding War Diaries and Intelligence Summaries are contained in F. S. Regs., Part II. and the Staff Manual respectively. Title pages will be prepared in manuscript.

Page 73

Hour, Date, Place	Summary of Events and Information	Remarks and references to Appendices
WESTOUTRE. 1915. August 19th	Detachment of 37" Div Gehst Coy reconnoitred country to the north as far as VLAMERTINGHE & to the South as far as NEUVE EGLISE _	2.
August 20"	8 am No 2 Platoon under Lieut Burge continued work on WULVERGHEN. Switch _ No. 6 Platoon employed for the day under the D.A.D.O.S. Detachment of 2 officers & 30 men 37" Div Gehst Coy relieved by another detachment of one officer & 30 OR 37" Div Gehst Coy _	Da
August 21"	8 am No 3 Platoon under Lieut Hawkins with detachment of 37" Div Gehst Coy. continued work on WULVERGHEN Switch _ No 4 Platoon under Lieut Williams employed digging in telephone wire at N. 14 a 5.0.	Fa.

WAR DIARY
or
INTELLIGENCE SUMMARY

(Erase heading not required.)

Army Form C. 2118.

Instructions regarding War Diaries and Intelligence
Summaries are contained in F. S. Regs., Part II.
and the Staff Manual respectively.   Title pages
will be prepared in manuscript.

Hour, Date, Place	Summary of Events and Information	Remarks and references to Appendices
WESTOUTRE 1915		
August 22 -	No 5 Platoon under Lieut Dalton continued work on WULVERGHEN switch -	
	No 6 Platoon under Lieut Phillips digging in telephone wire — work completed	
	Detachment 37 Div. Cyclist Co. reconnoitred country in vicinity of VLAMERTINGHE -	A.
August 23rd	No 2 Platoon under Lieut Burge continued work on WULVERGHEN switch —	A
	No 5 Platoon under Lt Dalton reconnoitred Battalion Hd Qrs of 83rd Brigade	
	No 6 Platoon reconnoitred Bn HdQrs of 84th Brigade	A.
August 24	Nos 3 & 4 Platoon under Lt Williams continued work of WULVERGHEN switch -	
	37 Div Cyclist Detachment rejoined their Company	A

WAR DIARY
or
INTELLIGENCE SUMMARY

(Erase heading not required.)

Army Form C. 2118.

Instructions regarding War Diaries and Intelligence
Summaries are contained in F. S. Regs., Part II.
and the Staff Manual respectively. Title pages
will be prepared in manuscript.

Page 75.

Hour, Date, Place	Summary of Events and Information	Remarks and references to Appendices
WESTOUTRE 1915. August 25. 8am. to 4pm	No. 5 + 6 Platoons under Lt Phillips continued work on WULVERGHEN switch —	
8am. to 4.30pm	No 2 Platoon under Lt Burge employed digging in telephone wire on Mt KUMMEL	Fa.
August 26 - 8am.	Nos. 3 + 4 Platoons under Lieut Williams - continued work on WULVERGHEN switch —	Fa.
7pm	15 N.C.Os. + men of No. 2 platoon under Lieut. Burge reconnoitred the Bn Hqrs of 84th Bde.	M.
August 27th 8am. to 4pm.	Nos. 5 + 6 platoons under Lieut. Phillips + Lieut Dalton continued work on WULVERGHEM trench line	M.
August 28th 8am to 3.15pm	Nos. 2 and 3 platoons under Lieut. Burge continued work on WULVERGHEM switch trenches.	M.
August 29th 8am	Nos. 4 + 5 platoons under Lieut Williams + Lieut Dalton continued work on WULVERGHEM switch trenches.	M.
	15 N.C.Os. + men of No 6 platoon visited Bn Hqrs of 83rd Bde	M.

WAR DIARY
or
INTELLIGENCE SUMMARY *M.D.*

(Erase heading not required.)

Army Form C. 2118.

Instructions regarding War Diaries and Intelligence Summaries are contained in F. S. Regs., Part II. and the Staff Manual respectively. Title pages will be prepared in manuscript.

Hour, Date, Place	Summary of Events and Information	Remarks and references to Appendices
WESTOUTRE 1915 August. 30th	*under Lieuts Burge & Phillips* 8am N° 6 and 2 platoons, continued work of digging 4pm. on WULVERGHEM switch trenches. *N° 5 platoon* 7.30pm. 15 N.C.O's & men, under Lieut Dalton reconnoitred the Bn Hqs. of 84th Bde.	M.D. M.D.
August 31st 8 am to 4.15pm	N° 3 platoon under Lieut Packard continued the work on WULVERGHEM switch trenches.	
(in the field) 1-9-15		

J.S.Wright
Comdg. 28th Div Cyclist Coy

28th Division

$\dfrac{121}{699}$ Y

28th Cyclist Coy

Vol IX

Sept. 15

Instructions regarding War Diaries and Intelligence
Summaries are contained in F. S. Regs., Part II.
and the Staff Manual respectively.   Title pages
will be prepared in manuscript.

(Erase heading not required.)

Hour, Date, Place	Summary of Events and Information	Remarks and references to Appendices
Page 77		
WESTOUTRE 1915.	No. 5 platoon under Lieut Dalton continued work on WULVERGHEM switch trenches.	
September 1st 8 a.m. to 4.15 p.m.	14 N.C.Os & 49 men of Nos. 2 + 4 platoons under Lieut. William detailed to control entrance & exit to the 'forbidden zone' viz the line of Franco - Belgian frontier. The following 6 standing patrol were posted :-	
12 noon	No. 19. at cross roads on LOCRE - BAILLEUL road 250ˣ S. of LOCRE CHᵃˢ	Ref. Belgian Sheet No. 28 40,000.
	20. at cross roads 400ˣ E. of LOCRE CHᵃˢ	
	21. at farm in track 300ˣ S. of Chaple on MONT VIDAIGNE	
	22 at cross roads near AU LUXEMBOURG Cᵃᴮᵀ on MONT NOIR	
	23 at cross roads 200ˣ N. of T in PUDEFORT	
	24 at cross roads 700ˣ N. of P in PUDEFORT	
	No. 2 platoon, finding Nos. 19, 20, & 21 posts billeted at farm 300 yards from No. 21 post.	M.P.
September 2nd 8 a.m.	No. 6 platoon under Lieut. Phillips continued work on WULVERGHEM switch trenches	
to 4.30 p.m.	Capt. Agg appointed Staff Capt. 28th Bde, left the unit and handed over command to Lieut. Packard.	M.P.
10 a.m.	No. 3 platoon under Lieut Dalton continued work on WULVERGHEM trenches. The work on support line [was complete]	M.P.
left 3rd 8 a.m.		

1247 W 3299 200,000 (E) 8/14 J.B.C. & A.   Forms/C. 2118/11.

WAR DIARY
or
INTELLIGENCE SUMMARY

Army Form C. 2118.

Instructions regarding War Diaries and Intelligence
Summaries are contained in F. S. Regs., Part II.
and the Staff Manual respectively. Title pages
will be prepared in manuscript.

(Erase heading not required.)

Hour, Date, Place	Summary of Events and Information	Remarks and references to Appendices
Page 78 WESTOUTRE — 1915 September 4th 7 am to 4.30 pm	No. 5 platoon under Lieut. Briggs continued work on firing line of WULVERGHEM outlet trenches	M8
5th 8 am to 4.30 pm	No. 6 platoon under Lieut. Phillips continued & completed the work allotted on the fire trenches of the WULVERGHEM outlet trench line.	M8
6th 8 am to 4.30 pm	No. 3 platoon under Lieut. Hopkins continued work on WULVERGHEM switch trenches. Another frontier control post was required & posted on LOCRE BAILLEUL road about ¼ mi. S.W. of No. 19 post. Total number of men now employed on frontier control posts — 1 officer & 79 men	M8
7th 8 am to 4.30 pm	Lieut. Walton took digging party of 1 Sergt & 20 men & continued work on WULVERGHEM outlet trenches. SCHERPENBERG was shelled during day. No casualties among guard, who but Lieut. Park was wounded during the day.	M8
8th 8 am to 4.30 pm 9.30 am	Lieut. Phillips took digging party of 1 sergt & 20 men & work on WULVERGHEM trenches. Moved the unit to billet in farm opposite LOCRE CHATEAU	M8

WAR DIARY
or
INTELLIGENCE SUMMARY.

Army Form C. 2118.

Instructions regarding War Diaries and Intelligence Summaries are contained in F. S. Regs., Part II. and the Staff Manual respectively. Title pages will be prepared in manuscript.

(Erase heading not required.)

Place	Date 1915	Hour	Summary of Events and Information	Remarks and references to Appendices
LOCRE	Sept. 9th	7.30 am	One Lance Sergt. and 15 men detailed &report to Camp Commandant BAILLEUL at 9 am. for work on roads — Men attached to Hqs II Corps.	
		8.15am to 4.15pm	Lieut. Hawkins took digging party of 1 Sergt. & 20 men to work on the WULVERGHEM trenches.	M.P.
	Sept. 10th	8.15 am to 4 pm	Lieut. Dalton took digging party of 1 sergt. & 20 men to continue work on the WULVERGHEM switch trenches.	M.P.
	Sept. 11th	8.15am to 4 pm	Lieut. Phillips took digging party of 1 sergt. & 20 men to work on VIERSTRAAT switch trenches — worked on line in neighbourhood of LA POLKA.	M.P.
	Sept. 12th	8.15am to 4 pm	Lieut. Hawkins took digging party of 1 sergt. & 20 men to work on VIERSTRAAT switch trenches in same locality as previous day	M.P.
	Sept. 13th	8.15am to 4.30pm	Lieut. Dalton took digging party of 1 Sergt. & 20 men to work on VIERSTRAAT switch trenches. and completed work assigned to him on that line	M.P.
	Sept. 14th	noon	Received reinforcement of 1 man, returned from base hospital — Nothing further to report	M.P.

1577 Wt. W10791/1773 500,000 1/15 D. D. & L.   A.D.S.S./Forms/C. 2118.

WAR DIARY
or
INTELLIGENCE SUMMARY.
(Erase heading not required.)

Army Form C. 21

Instructions regarding War Diaries and Intelligence
Summaries are contained in F. S. Regs., Part II.
and the Staff Manual respectively. Title pages
will be prepared in manuscript.

Page 80

Place	Date 1915	Hour	Summary of Events and Information	Remarks and references to Appendices
LOCRE	Sept. 15th		Nothing to report	1 AW
	16th		Nothing to report	1 AW
	17th		Nothing to report.	1 AW
	18th		2 Lieut. C. H. D. Bonnett joined the company for duty, and took over No 2 platoon	1 AW
	19th	8am to 5 pm	A fatigue party of 1 sergt & 15 men sent to work under C.R.E at the Divl R.E Park	1 AW
	20th	7.30 am	Lieut. C. G. Burge left the company to join Royal Flying Corps Headquarters.	
		10 am	No 3 platoon relieved No 1 platoon at Divisional Headquarters.	
		2 to 6.55 pm	A fatigue party of 1 sergt & 15 men sent to work at Divl RE park.	
		8 pm	Picquet of 1 n.c.o. & 3 men sent to Divl RE park by request of C.R.E.	
			During the day 2nd Canadian Divl Cyclists arrived & bivouacked near the billets of the company. Handed over control posts on Franco-Belgian frontier to Canadian Divl Cyclists at 4 pm	1 AW
	21st	8 am	Fatigue party of 1 sergt & 15 men sent to R.E. Park as previous day	
		9 am	Lieut. Daniel, Lieut Philips & Lieut Dalton took small parties of 2nd Canadian Divl Cyclists to 13th 14th and 15th Inf. Bde Hqs and to	

WAR DIARY

or

INTELLIGENCE SUMMARY.

(*Erase heading not required.*)

Army Form C. 21

Instructions regarding War Diaries and Intelligence
Summaries are contained in F. S. Regs., Part II.
and the Staff Manual respectively. Title pages
will be prepared in manuscript.

Place	Date 1915	Hour	Summary of Events and Information	Remarks and references to Appendices
LOCRE	Sept 21st (cont'd)		some Bttn Hqrs so that they should learn the country in rear of the firing line.	
		4 pm	Handed over SCHERPENBERG guard, to 2nd Canadian Divn Cyclists.	M.M.
MERRIS	22nd	10 am	Moved the unit to billets in new Divnl Area, at farm 200 yds N. of E in MERRIS	Ref: HAZEBROUCK Map 5 A.
		11.30am	Arrived in new billets.	
		6 pm	Party of 1 Usergt & 15 men returned from work under II Corps at BAILLEUL	M.M.
	23rd	6 pm	Ordered to be prepared to move at one hours notice.	M.M.
	24th		Nothing to report.	M.M.
	25th	6 pm	Ordered to be prepared to move at 2 hours notice.	M.M.
	26th	6.30am	Left billets to reach starting point of column at 7.30 am, 1 mile S. of MERRIS	
		8.0am	Continued march via VIEUX BERQUIN and NEUF BERQUIN to MERVILLE	

WAR DIARY
or
INTELLIGENCE SUMMARY.

Army Form C. 2118.

Instructions regarding War Diaries and Intelligence
Summaries are contained in F. S. Regs., Part II.
and the Staff Manual respectively. Title pages
will be prepared in manuscript.

(*Erase heading not required.*)

Place	Date 1915	Hour	Summary of Events and Information	Remarks and references to Appendices
MERVILLE	26th (oct)	12 noon	Arrived at MERVILLE and proceeded to billet on MERVILLE - REGNIER road	
		2 pm	Received orders to resume march towards BETHUNE at 2.15 pm. Marched via PARADIS and LOCON	
BETHUNE		10 pm	Arrived at BETHUNE and billeted at Skating Rink in RUE de GENDARMERIE, with B Sqn Surrey Yeomanry.	J.W.W.
	27th		Nothing to report	
	28th	10.30 am	Lieut. Dalton, 12 N.C.O's & 47 men from Nos. 2, 4, and 5 platoons proceeded to SAILLY LA BOURSE for work under A.P.M 28th Divn. finding straggler posts, road control etc	[Ref. Map 36 B 1/40,000. B series]
		4.45 pm	Lieut. Philips, Lieut Bonnell, and Lieut. Hawkins, took a party of 70 ncos & men to CLARKES KEEP, VERMELLES to carry up bombs, ammunition, rations etc to units of 85th Inf. Bde. returned to billets between 5 and 6 am on 29th inst. Casualties one lance corporal accidentally injured	J.W.W.

WAR DIARY
or
INTELLIGENCE SUMMARY. *MW*

(Erase heading not required.)

Army Form C. 2118.

Instructions regarding War Diaries and Intelligence
Summaries are contained in F. S. Regs., Part II.
and the Staff Manual respectively. Title pages
will be prepared in manuscript.

Place Page 83.	Date	Hour	Summary of Events and Information	Remarks and references to Appendices
BÉTHUNE	Sept.29ᵗʰ	1 pm	Ordered to bring all available men of company to Divⁿ Hqʳˢ at CHᵃᵘ des PRES, SAILLY LA BOURSE.	
		2 pm	Lieut. WILLIAMS took a party of 2 officers (Lieut Phillips & Lieut. Hawkins) and 62 n.c.o's and men to establish and maintain a bomb depot for 85ᵗʰ Inf Bde & 83ʳᵈ Inf Bde if necessary at BARTS, on railway line N.E. of VERMELLES [Ref Trench Map 36 C N.W. 3 and part of 1 – at point G 3 C 6.6].	MW
		5 pm	1 n.c.o. & 2 men accompanied limbered wagon with rations – great coats etc – for above party.	
		7 pm	Lieut. PHILLIPS returned.	
	30ᵗʰ	2 pm	I visited bomb depot at BARTS, bringing Lieut. Daniel and Lieut Bonnett to relieve Lieut. Williams and Lieut. Hawkins. A good supply of bombs was kept up during the day – from 8 am onwards the number at BARTS amounted to over 1,000 bombs.	
		4 pm	limbered waggon & ration party left for CLARKES KEEP. VERMELLES. returned to billets at about 10 pm.	

J E.E. Packard Capt.
Cmdg 28ᵗʰ Divⁿ Cyclist Coy.

1577 Wt. W10791/1773 500,000 1/15 D. D. & L. A.D.S.S./Forms/C. 2118.

Volume No. IX

121
Medii
019

MEDITERRANEAN EXPEDITIONARY FORCE.

WAR DIARY.

28th Div France

Unit 28th Division Cyclist Coy.

From 1st October 1915. To 31st October 1915.

Left France 26 Law
Alexandria 31/?
&

Instructions regarding War Diaries and Intelligence
Summaries are contained in F. S. Regs., Part II.
and the Staff Manual respectively. Title pages
will be prepared in manuscript.

Place 84. Page 84.	Date 1915	Hour	Summary of Events and Information	Remarks and references to Appendices
BETHUNE	Oct 1st	8 am	Sent baggage waggon to CLARKES KEEP – VERMELLES with mens packs & Kit, cooks utensils etc.	*MW*
		2.30 pm	Lieut. Phillips & Lieut. Hawkins left to relieve Lieut. Daniel & Lieut. Bonnett at CLARKES KEEP.	
	2nd	10 am	I visited Lieut. Dalton's party under A.P.M. 28th Division.	*MW* cut off
		2.30 pm	Lieut. Daniel & Lieut. Bonnett *& 45 men* relieved Lieut. Phillips & Lieut Hawkins at CLARKES KEEP. Lieut. Daniel delivered a large supply of bombs to 2 coys. of Northd Fusiliers who were *cut off from their unit.*	
	3rd	8 am	Sent a party of 3 N.C.Os and 9 men to relieve a corresponding party at CLARKES KEEP	
		3 pm	Lieut. Williams & Lieut. Phillips relieved Lieut. Daniel and Lieut. Bonnett at CLARKES KEEP. BARTS bomb store handed over to Staff Capt. 83rd Brigade.	*MW*
		3.30 pm	Moved unit headquarters to farm S.E. of BEUVRY.	
BEUVRY	4th	11 am	I reported with all available men to Major Hope. D.A.Q.M.G. 28th Dvn at CLARKES KEEP for special work	
		12.30 pm	Lieut. Williams and 32 ncos & men carried ammunition and accessories for the	

1577 Wt. W10791/1773 500,000 1/15 D. D. & L.   A.D.S.S./Forms/C. 2118.

WAR DIARY
or
INTELLIGENCE SUMMARY. JW

Army Form C. 2118.

Instructions regarding War Diaries and Intelligence Summaries are contained in F. S. Regs., Part II. and the Staff Manual respectively. Title pages will be prepared in manuscript.

(Erase heading not required.)

Place	Date 1915.	Hour	Summary of Events and Information	Remarks and references to Appendices
BEUVRY	Oct 4th (contd)		STOKES Trench Mortar Battery to their position in front line trenches.	
		2 pm	Lieut. Phillips & 18 men and a party of Surrey Yeomanry took trench mortar and smoke bomb ammunition and accessories to their position in front line trenches	
		5 pm	Both parties returned, having salvaged about 60 spare rifles and sets of equipment. handing them over to Staff Capt. 83rd Brigade	
		6.15 pm	Lieut. Daniel & Lieut. Hawkins relieved Lieut. William & Lieut. Phillips at CLARKES KEEP. I returned with them to billets at BEUVRY	
		7.30 pm	Lieut. Daniel & 20 men buried 10 bodies in neighbourhood of 83rd Bde Hqrs. in CENTRAL BOYAU, and salvaged more rifles & equipment. Casualties 1 man wounded.	
		8 pm	Lieut. Hawkins & 35 men took bombs to 2nd King's Own Regt.	JW
	Oct 5th	1 am	Above parties completed work at about 1 am.	
		1.30 pm	Received orders to move to rest Area BUSNES – GOONNEHEM – Ordered Lieut. Daniel to return from VERMELLES to BEUVRY with all his men Sent limbered waggon to VERMELLES to field kits and cooks utensils.	
		3.30 pm	Lieut. Daniel's party returned.	

1577 Wt. W10791/1773 500,000 1/15 D. D. & L. A.D.S.S./Forms/C. 2118.

WAR DIARY

or

INTELLIGENCE SUMMARY. *Ind*

(*Erase heading not required.*)

Army Form C. 2118.

Instructions regarding War Diaries and Intelligence
Summaries are contained in F. S. Regs., Part II.
and the Staff Manual respectively. Title pages
will be prepared in manuscript.

Place	Date 1915	Hour	Summary of Events and Information	Remarks and references to Appendices
BEUVRY	Oct 5th (cont'd)	5.30pm	Limbered waggon returned with Kits.	
		6.pm	Left BEUVRY and proceeded via BETHUNE - CHOCQUES - GONNEHEM - L'ÉCLEME. BUSNES to billets 200 x S of C. in LE CORNET BRASSARD. distance 14½ miles. arriving at 10.30pm Transport arrived at 12 midnight.	J.M.V.
BUSNES [LE CORNET BRASSARD]	Oct 6th		Rest area. Baths obtained for men. cleaning up.	Ind
	7th		Nothing to report.	Ind
	8th		Inspected by G.O.C. 1st Corps. on parade with R.E. and Surrey Yeomanry. in a field N.E. of BUSNES.	Ind
	9th		Company visited by G.O.C. 28th Divn	Ind
	10th		Church parade.	Ind

Instructions regarding War Diaries and Intelligence Summaries are contained in F. S. Regs., Part II. and the Staff Manual respectively. Title pages will be prepared in manuscript.

WAR DIARY
or
INTELLIGENCE SUMMARY

(Erase heading not required.)

Army Form C. 2118.

Place	Date 1915	Hour	Summary of Events and Information	Remarks and references to Appendices
BUSNES [LE CORNET BRASSARD]	Oct. 11th		Nothing to report.	
	–12th		Nothing to report.	
	13th		Nothing to report.	
	14th		Lt. J. S. JONES-SAVIN, Army. Cyclist Corps joined the company for duty from training centre.	
	15th		Nothing to report	
	16th	11 am	Inspected by General BRIGGS, G.O.C. 28th Divn.	
	17th	9 am	Lieut DANIEL and patrol located Hq's of units of 83rd Inf Bde. in trenches, and reconnoitred commn trenches.	
		11 am.	Moved unit at 11 am. to BETHUNE; obtained temporary billets in building near ORPHANAGE in RUE DE LILLE.	

1577 Wt. W10791/1773 500,000 1/15 D. D. & L.   A.D.S.S./Forms/C. 2118.

WAR DIARY
or
INTELLIGENCE SUMMARY.

Army Form C. 2118.

Instructions regarding War Diaries and Intelligence
Summaries are contained in F. S. Regs., Part II.
and the Staff Manual respectively. Title pages
will be prepared in manuscript.

(Erase heading not required.)

Place	Date 1915	Hour	Summary of Events and Information	Remarks and references to Appendices
BETHUNE	Oct. 18th	10 am	A patrol of 2 ncos + 2 men went to 83rd Bde Area. visiting headquarters of units. and making themselves acquainted with comm comm trenches leading to them.	
			A patrol of 1 ncos + 1 man went to 85th Bde Area. locating hqs of units	
		1 pm	Both patrols returned	
	19th	10.30 am	Moved unit in to TOBACCO FACTORY in RUE DE LILLE	
		2 pm	LIEUT. PHILLIPS and patrol went to 85th Bde Area locating headquarters of units in the trenches + making themselves acquainted with comm trenches leading to them. returned 5.30 pm.	
			A patrol of 1 ncos + 1 man went to 84th Bde area. locating hqs. of units returned 5 pm	
	20th		Nothing to report.	
	21st		Received orders to entrain at LILLERS Stn by train leaving 18.51. (6.51 pm)	
		2 pm	Left BETHUNE.	
		4 pm	arrived LILLERS.	

1577 Wt. W10791/1773 500,000 1/15 D.D. & L.   A.D.S.S./Forms/C. 2118.

WAR DIARY
or
INTELLIGENCE SUMMARY.

Army Form C. 2118.

Instructions regarding War Diaries and Intelligence Summaries are contained in F. S. Regs., Part II. and the Staff Manual respectively. Title pages will be prepared in manuscript.

(Erase heading not required.)

Place	Date 1915	Hour	Summary of Events and Information	Remarks and references to Appendices
LILLERS	Oct. 21	5.30pm	Commenced to entrain. 3 L.D. Horses & drivers for same had to be left behind to come by next train. All second line transport waggon returned to Train Coy.	JMP
		7.30	Train left LILLERS.	
In train	22nd	—	Train Route. St POL – St DENIS – MONTARGIS. halted twice for meals & tea for men	JMP
	23rd	—	Train route LYON – AVIGNON – MARSEILLES. halted twice for meals	JMP
MARSEILLES	24th	2.30am	Arrived at quai side. Detrained. Marched to boat.	JMP
		4.30am	Embarked on H.T ROYAL GEORGE	JMP
	25th	11.30am	H.T ROYAL GEORGE sailed for unknown destination	JMP
	26th – 30th	—	At Sea.	JMP

1577 Wt. W10791/1773 500,000 1/15 D. D. & L. A.D.S.S./Forms/C. 2118.

WAR DIARY
or
INTELLIGENCE SUMMARY.

(Erase heading not required.)

Army Form C. 2118.

Instructions regarding War Diaries and Intelligence Summaries are contained in F. S. Regs., Part II. and the Staff Manual respectively. Title pages will be prepared in manuscript.

Place	Date	Hour	Summary of Events and Information	Remarks and references to Appendices
	1915.			
ALEXANDRIA	31st Oct.	2.30 pm	Company disembarked at ALEXANDRIA – marched to VICTORIA COLLEGE CAMP at SIDI BISHR.	1118
SIDI BISHR		4 pm	pitched Camp.	
			J.E.E. Packard Capt. cmdg 28th Divl Cyclist Coy.	
	1-11-15.			

1577 Wt. W10791/1773 500,000 1/15 D. D. & L. A.D.S.S./Forms/C. 2118.